Healing Your Wounded Inner Child

A comprehensive guide to overcome past trauma, abuse and abandonment

Stella Nash

Table of Contents

ISBN Number : 978-93-341-2816-1

Introduction

As a child, the hands that should have held me with care became the ones that inflicted the most harm. The people I depended on for love and protection instead delivered pain— physical abuse that left bruises and emotional wounds that ran even deeper. In a place where I should have felt safe, I was instead trapped in a world of fear, where every day was a struggle to survive. This trauma shaped my view of the world, leaving me to believe that love had to be earned through obedience and silence, and that vulnerability was something to be feared.

In adulthood, this pain manifested as aggressive, dominating behavior. I became controlling in relationships, lashing out at anyone who challenged me, afraid that if I wasn't in control, I would be hurt again. At work, my abrasive nature pushed people away, though it masked deep feelings of inadequacy. It took years of broken relationships and heartache before I realized that my aggression was not strength, but a defense mechanism, shielding the wounded child within me.

My need for control and my harsh reactions were driving people away, reinforcing the very isolation and pain I was trying to avoid. Through inner child work, I learned to heal, let go of the need for control, and embrace vulnerability. As I healed, my relationships deepened, and I began to live with more peace, love, and self-compassion.

I still remember the day I unearthed my old stuffed rabbit. As I held it close, it struck me how this simple toy represented the innocence I had lost. It was in that moment I realized: healing the wounded inner child would be my path to reclaiming joy - and that my life path would be to help others heal as well.

This book is born out of countless such moments—small epiphanies and deep reflections that revealed the profound influence our childhood experiences have on our present lives. My journey mirrors many others who grapple with the lingering effects of early emotional wounds, experiencing struggles that seem insurmountable yet deeply yearning for healing and personal growth.

The inner child is the part of us that holds our memories, emotions, and experiences from childhood. It reflects our purest essence and can be an essential ally in overcoming the shadows of our past. Understanding this part of ourselves is crucial to our healing journey. Imagine holding onto a piece of your history that has the power to unlock not only the pains of your past but also the potential joys of your future. The inner child represents our innocence, spontaneity, and capacity for joy, often buried beneath layers of adult responsibilities and unresolved pain.

Many of us carry invisible scars from our childhood—scars that interfere with our relationships, self-esteem, and daily lives. You may find yourself wondering, "Why do I react this way?" or "Why can't I feel happy?" These questions are common, but they also mark the start of a transformative journey. Perhaps you've felt like something is missing, or you struggle to form healthy relationships despite your best efforts. These challenges are more widespread than you might think.

For survivors of childhood trauma and abuse, these struggles can feel especially acute. The lingering emotions and reactions rooted in painful experiences can create a sense of isolation and frustration. It's important to know that these feelings are valid and shared by many who walk this path. You're not alone in your fears, your sadness, or your hope for something better. Acknowledging these common struggles helps us see that our experiences, while unique in their details, resonate on a fundamental level with countless others.

Imagine a life where you can navigate relationships with confidence and express your emotions freely. Healing your inner child isn't just about addressing past trauma; it's about unlocking a future filled with joy, authenticity, and resilience. The journey may be long, but the promise of healing awaits you. This book aims to illuminate that path, offering not just insights but actionable tools to help you through the process.

Healing is neither linear nor easy. It involves revisiting painful memories and confronting uncomfortable truths. Yet, the rewards are immeasurable. By understanding and nurturing your inner child, you open up possibilities for deeper connections, greater self-awareness, and a renewed sense of purpose. Every step taken towards healing is a step towards reclaiming parts of yourself you've forgotten or suppressed.

For those experiencing relationship challenges linked to unresolved emotional wounds, this book will serve as a guide. Navigating relationships when carrying the weight of past traumas can feel like an insurmountable challenge. Emotional intelligence, the ability to understand and manage your own emotions and those of others, is key to forming healthier and more fulfilling relationships. You'll find strategies here to improve this skill, fostering stronger, more empathetic connections with others.

The process of healing and self-discovery is deeply personal, but it's also one that thrives on community and shared understanding. By connecting with others who share similar experiences, you can find strength in solidarity, learn from diverse perspectives, and gain encouragement when the path seems daunting. This sense of communal support can be incredibly empowering, reminding you that you don't have to face these challenges alone.

Throughout the book, you'll encounter real stories from individuals who have walked this difficult path and emerged stronger and more authentic. Their journeys illustrate the power of healing and offer inspiration and practical advice. These narratives, combined with exercises and reflections, will help you engage actively with the material, applying it in ways that resonate most with your unique experiences.

As you embark on this journey, remember to be gentle with yourself. Healing takes time, and every small step forward is progress worth celebrating.

Embrace the process with an open heart, allowing room for both setbacks and victories. Your inner child, once acknowledged and healed, can become a source of immense strength and joy.

Ultimately, this book is about transformation—not just of how you perceive your past, but how you envision your future. It's about breaking free from the chains of past wounds and stepping into a future where you can live fully and love deeply. Whether you're seeking to heal from childhood trauma or looking to improve your emotional intelligence and relationships, the path laid out here offers guidance, support, and hope.

Welcome to your journey of healing. Here's to rediscovering the parts of you that thrive on joy, connection, and authenticity. May this book be a beacon of light on your path to emotional freedom and personal development.

Understanding the Inner Child

> "The greatest wounds, we carry within our souls, are the ones that come from our childhood." – Graham Greene

In the realm of emotional well-being, understanding the inner child is crucial. This concept encompasses the emotions and impressions formed during your early years. The events of your childhood play a significant role in shaping your behavior, beliefs, and relationships as an adult. If you've faced trauma or find yourself struggling in your interactions, recognizing the impact of your inner child can be a powerful step toward healing and growth.

Definition and Origins of the Inner Child

In the middle of the 20th century, psychotherapy started looking at how childhood experiences affect adult behavior. This was a change from earlier psychology theories that mainly focused on conscious thoughts and actions. Acknowledging the subconscious influences like your inner child has been a significant advancement in the field.

Psychologists like John Bradshaw have explored the inner child deeply, showing how childhood pain from abuse or neglect affects your adult life. Bradshaw introduced approaches that focus on healing your inner child, emphasizing that unresolved issues can create psychological difficulties later on. It's crucial to face these lingering issues for better emotional health (CBT, 2014).

The idea of the inner child isn't just for individual therapy; it's part of various counseling methods. For example, cognitive-behavioral therapy (CBT) often addresses negative thinking patterns that stem from childhood experiences. By recognizing and challenging these patterns, CBT therapists help you understand the roots of your emotional struggles, paving the way to meaningful healing (Hestbech, 2018).

In this book, we will cover various techniques to help you reconnect with this aspect of yourself, encouraging the exploration of both joyful and painful memories to address unresolved emotions. Engaging in these exercises will validate your childhood feelings and create a supportive environment that may have been missing in your early life, helping you heal emotionally. Nurturing this connection with your inner child serves as a profound avenue for personal healing.

> One of the most successful and fulfilling cases of inner child healing I've worked on is Sophie, a woman in her forties whose chaotic childhood left deep scars. Growing up, she was constantly caught between her parents' explosive fights, feeling responsible for keeping the peace. Her emotions were dismissed, and she learned to suppress her feelings, believing her needs didn't matter.
>
> As an adult, Sophie feared conflict and became a people-pleaser, overextending herself to avoid disappointing others. Through our inner child work, Sophie reconnected with the scared child inside, realizing that her fear of conflict came from her upbringing. As she validated her emotions, she learned to set boundaries and prioritize her own needs.

> The change was remarkable—Sophie no longer avoided conflict and began embracing her true self, finding peace and self-worth. Watching her heal and transform was deeply rewarding for me.

Roles and Characteristics of the Inner Child

Before we move forward, let us understand the main aspects of the inner child and how they relate to you.

The **playful inner child** is the heart of your emotional development, embodying creativity, curiosity, and joy. This part of you connects with feelings of delight and playfulness. In your adult life, embracing this vibrant side can energize your spirit, encouraging freedom and spontaneity. Tapping into your playful inner child reignites your passions, dreams, and hidden talents often overshadowed by adult responsibilities. By rediscovering this aspect of yourself, you unlock a wellspring of creativity and joy that deeply enriches your life.

To nurture your playful inner child, it's vital to dedicate time to activities that spark happiness and fun, such as hobbies, sports, or games. Allowing yourself to engage fully in these pleasures without self-criticism lets you experience pure enjoyment, significantly boosting your overall well-being. This engagement encourages you to step back from your daily duties and relish light-hearted moments, fostering a healthy balance between work and leisure.

On the flip side, your **wounded inner child** represents the parts of you that have faced pain, fear, and unmet needs during childhood. These injuries can range from slight disappointments, like not receiving a toy you desired, to severe traumas such as emotional neglect or physical abuse. Recognizing and healing your wounded inner child is crucial for overcoming deep emotional scars. This aspect carries painful memories and unresolved trauma, which can show up as emotional challenges and behavioral issues in adulthood.

Healing your wounded inner child starts with acknowledging these past pains and validating the hurt they've caused. This process often involves self-reflection and, at times, seeking professional help to navigate complex emotions. Creating a safe space to explore these feelings is imperative. Methods like journaling, therapy, and guided meditations focused on inner child work can provide essential support. As you work through your emotional pain, you build self-esteem, improve how you manage your feelings, and create better relationships.

Equally important is the **nurturing inner child** , which promotes self-compassion and kindness. Engaging with this nurturing aspect is vital for building emotional resilience and effective coping strategies. By connecting with your nurturing inner child, you learn to offer yourself the care and empathy that may have been lacking during your early years. This self-compassion fosters a secure inner environment that supports emotional and mental growth.

Practicing regular self-care is key to nurturing your inner child. This can include comforting activities like enjoying a warm bath, diving into beloved books, or spending time in nature. Additionally, engaging in positive affirmations and mindfulness exercises can strengthen your compassionate relationship with yourself. Over time, these practices establish a solid emotional foundation, enhancing your ability to cope with stress and adversity.

Finally, the **inner critic** —often linked to the inner child—originates from negative experiences and critical feedback received during childhood. This inner voice can become a persistent source of self-doubt, fostering feelings of inadequacy and low self-worth. Understanding the roots of your inner critic is essential to diminishing its power and promoting greater self-acceptance.

To deal with your inner critic, identify the specific thoughts it creates. Once you know what these are, challenge them by questioning if they are true and replace them with positive statements. Changing your mindset takes practice, but with the techniques you'll learn in this book, it can be done and will greatly improve your self-esteem and mental well-being.

Recognizing the different parts of your inner child is important for your personal growth and healing. Your playful inner child brings joy and creativity, reminding you how fun and playful life can be. The wounded inner child shows that you need to deal with past hurts and unmet needs to heal emotionally. The nurturing inner child helps you be kind and compassionate, which is important for being strong and handling tough times. At the same time, dealing with your inner critic helps you overcome its negativity, leading to self-acceptance and better self-esteem.

Impact of Childhood Experiences on the Inner Child

Childhood experiences play a big role in shaping who you are and how you handle emotions as an adult. The people and situations you face when you're young can affect your emotional reactions later in life. For example, growing up in a loving and supportive home helps you feel safe and boosts your self-esteem, which leads to healthier emotional reactions in adulthood. On the other hand, a chaotic or neglectful upbringing can hurt your emotional growth, making it hard to manage feelings and form stable relationships as an adult.

Unresolved childhood trauma can affect your behavior as an adult. Trauma interrupts your natural emotional growth and can lead to unhealthy ways of coping. These strategies might provide temporary relief but can turn into hard-to-break habits. This might show up as trust issues, ongoing anxiety, or self-sabotage. Knowing how these past experiences influence your current actions and mental health is important.

Your early experiences shape how you connect with others. The way you interacted with caregivers and friends as a child affects your future relationships. If your main caregivers were emotionally distant or inconsistent, you might look for approval from others, which can lead to relying too much on them or feeling inadequate. On the other hand, positive childhood experiences and strong bonds give you a solid base for healthy relationships that are based on respect and trust. Understanding these patterns helps you address unhealthy behaviors and build stronger, more secure connections.

> Sarah is a great example of how childhood experiences affect adults. As a child, Sarah experienced emotional neglect from her parents, who were often preoccupied with their own struggles and failed to provide the love and support she craved. This unresolved trauma led her to develop a belief that she was unworthy of love and attention.
>
> As she grew into adulthood, Sarah found herself in a series of romantic relationships where she would constantly push her

partners away, convinced that they would eventually abandon her, just like her parents had. Despite her partners expressing love and commitment, she struggled to trust them, often sabotaging the relationships out of her own subconscious fear.

Sarah also dealt with persistent anxiety, worrying excessively about small things and feeling overwhelmed in social situations. Her coping strategies included excessive work and avoidance of personal connections, which provided temporary relief but ultimately left her feeling isolated and unfulfilled.

It wasn't until Sarah sought therapy that she began to understand the roots of her behavior and how her childhood trauma had shaped her adult life. By recognizing these patterns, she started to heal her inner child, practicing self-compassion and gradually learning to trust others again. Sarah's journey highlights the importance of addressing unresolved childhood trauma to foster emotional growth and build healthier relationships in adulthood.

Engaging with both happy and sad childhood memories is important for understanding and fixing ongoing emotional problems. Reflecting on these experiences helps you find out why you struggle today and opens doors to healing. Remembering good memories can bring back happiness and improve your self-esteem, while facing painful ones is necessary to recognize emotional pain that hasn't been resolved. By working through these experiences, you can start to heal your inner child and promote personal growth and emotional stability.

Specific practices, like mindfulness, can help when revisiting childhood memories. Mindfulness means being aware of your thoughts and feelings without judging them, which helps you face past experiences without feeling too stressed. Writing in a journal can also be a good way to express emotions and explore childhood memories. It gives you a clear way to understand your feelings, bringing out insights that you might not notice just by thinking alone. Therapy methods, like inner child work and EMDR (Eye Movement Desensitization and Reprocessing), provide guidance to help you deal with and heal deep-seated trauma.

Childhood behavioral patterns often persist into adulthood. For instance, if you learned to suppress your feelings to avoid conflict as a child, this may result in difficulties expressing emotions authentically in your adult life. Spotting these patterns is the first crucial step toward meaningful change. With deliberate effort and practice, you can discover healthier methods for responding to emotional triggers. Techniques from Cognitive Behavioral Therapy (CBT) are particularly effective in recognizing and adjusting these long-established habits, and we will apply them as we move ahead.

The coping methods you learned as a child help protect you from emotional pain. While these methods were important for getting through tough times, they can make it hard to form real emotional connections and grow as an adult. Actions like avoiding problems, denying feelings, or pushing them down can interfere with true experiences. Learning to overcome these habits takes time and being kind to yourself. Techniques like mindfulness and gradually facing what you fear can help decrease the use of these old defenses, allowing for a more genuine emotional life.

The way you view yourself comes from your childhood experiences. What you were told about your worth and abilities shapes how you see yourself today. If you faced a lot of criticism as a child, it can make you feel like you're not good enough or have low self-esteem. On the other hand, support and praise help you build a strong and positive self-image. To improve your self-image as an adult, you need to challenge the negative beliefs you developed as a child and replace them with positive thoughts that encourage self-kindness and acceptance.

Building better relationships means understanding why you behave a certain way and trying to change it. Knowing what triggers your feelings and reactions—many of which come from your past—helps you interact in a more thoughtful way. Listening actively, setting boundaries, and clearly saying what you need are important for creating healthier and more meaningful connections. Taking time to reflect on your thoughts and asking for advice from people you trust can also improve your social skills, leading to stronger connections based on understanding and respect.

Concluding Thoughts

Healing your inner child is essential for your emotional well-being. It's important to understand how your childhood experiences influence your adult behavior, perceptions, and relationships. By examining the different aspects of your inner child —the playful spirit, the wounded self, the nurturing figure, and the inner critic—you can uncover their significant roles in your emotional growth. Acknowledging these elements and addressing unresolved traumas will allow you to enhance your emotional health and build stronger, more meaningful connections.

As you delve deeper into the impact of your early experiences on your current life, the next chapter will provide practical strategies for identifying childhood traumas and starting your journey toward healing.

Identifying Childhood Traumas

> "Until you make the unconscious conscious, it will direct your life and you will call it fate." - Carl Jung

Identifying childhood traumas is a powerful step toward understanding how early experiences shape our lives. These traumas often leave lasting marks, influencing our emotional responses, behaviors, and relationships in ways we might not immediately recognize. For many, the pains of the past continue to whisper through the decades, echoing in moments of anxiety, depression, or even unexplained physical pain. Acknowledging these experiences is about more than revisiting painful memories; it's about breaking free from their unseen hold on our daily lives and beginning the journey toward healing and self-discovery.

Types of Childhood Trauma: Abuse, Neglect, Abandonment

Childhood traumas can take many forms, such as physical, emotional, or sexual abuse, along with emotional and physical neglect and abandonment. By recognizing and naming these traumas, you can embark on your healing journey.

Physical abuse is often the most recognizable trauma. It encompasses any intentional harm to a child through physical contact, including hitting, beating, burning or other forms of physical harm. While the immediate consequences are visible—like bruises and fractures—the long-term effects loom larger, manifesting as chronic pain and a heightened risk of mental health challenges such as depression, anxiety, and PTSD.

Emotional abuse, though less obvious, can be just as harmful. It includes actions that undermine a child's self-esteem or emotional health, such as verbal insults, humiliation, intimidation, or consistent criticism. Such abuse can profoundly influence a child's growth, leading to low self-worth, difficulties in building healthy relationships, and challenges in managing emotions. Studies have indicated that emotional maltreatment can be a stronger predictor of psychological disorders in adulthood than physical abuse (Lippard & Nemeroff, 2019).

Sexual abuse is a harrowing type of trauma where a child is involved in any sexual activity without the ability to consent. This encompasses both direct actions, like molestation, and indirect ones, such as exposure to inappropriate sexual content. Survivors often endure lasting effects into adulthood, grappling with intense feelings of shame, guilt, relationship struggles, and an increased vulnerability to conditions like PTSD and depression.

Neglect, whether emotional or physical, occurs when a caregiver fails to fulfill a child's essential needs. Physical neglect relates to inadequate provision of food, clothing, or medical care, while emotional neglect stems from a caregiver's lack of emotional presence, producing a void of affection and support. Children who face neglect frequently experience developmental delays and psychological challenges, impacting their capacity to trust, form attachments, and manage anxiety and depressive symptoms.

Abandonment trauma can manifest as either physical or emotional. Physical abandonment entails a caregiver leaving a child without adequate supervision, which can create immediate hazards and long-lasting fears about safety. Emotional abandonment occurs when caregivers are emotionally unavailable or reject their child, instilling feelings of neglect and unworthiness. This results in deep-seated fears of insecurity and abandonment in future relationships.

Understanding these various trauma types is vital, as it allows you to grasp how your past influences your current feelings and behaviors. Each trauma type presents its own unique challenges, necessitating tailored approaches to healing. For instance, if you've experienced physical abuse, therapies that promote body awareness and safety may be beneficial, while a survivor of emotional neglect might need to focus on rebuilding self-esteem and emotional expression.

Identifying the specifics of your trauma can significantly enhance your healing journey. By naming and acknowledging your experiences, you create a pathway to effectively address these wounds. Understanding the root of your pain enables you to seek therapeutic methods and support systems that meet your individual needs.

The importance of acknowledging and comprehending your trauma cannot be emphasized enough. It sheds light on what might otherwise be a confusing mix of symptoms and reactions. Understanding the precise nature of your childhood traumas helps you uncover the foundational causes of certain behaviors and emotional responses.

Common Symptoms of Unresolved Childhood Trauma

Childhood trauma can leave deep marks on your life, often surfacing in ways that may catch you off guard. Recognizing how those early experiences influence your emotional, behavioral, relational, and physical health as an adult is crucial for healing and growth.

One clear sign that childhood trauma still impacts you today is found in your emotional reactions. Continued feelings of anxiety, sadness, and anger often originate from past traumatic experiences. Anxiety may feel like a constant unease or fear, ignited by events in your current life that seem unrelated. Depression can manifest as ongoing dullness, lack of energy, or disinterest in activities you once loved. Anger, frequently misunderstood, acts as a shield against discomfort or fear. Acknowledging these feelings as signals of past trauma, rather than unrelated episodes, can be a significant insight.

Your behaviors also reflect unresolved trauma. For many, turning to substances like alcohol or drugs becomes a way to cope. These may offer temporary escape but end up worsening underlying issues. Similarly, self-sabotage—whether in professional pursuits, personal projects, or relationships—often arises from feelings of inadequacy or fear of failing that were instilled during your development. By recognizing these behaviors, you can look deeper to uncover the emotions they conceal.

Childhood trauma casts a long shadow on your relationships. Trust issues may surface, where even minor offenses trigger disproportionate reactions, leading to a reluctance to form close ties or a desperate need for validation. You might find intimacy intimidating; vulnerability in close relationships can feel overwhelmingly risky if your past involved betrayal or harm. As a result, you may either shy away from deep connections or gravitate towards relationships that repeat patterns of dysfunction.

Physical signs of trauma can also be revealing. Chronic pain might persist without any clear medical explanation, stemming from your body's prolonged response to stress. Psychosomatic symptoms—where emotional distress manifests physically—are not uncommon. These may present as headaches, digestive issues, or unexplained discomfort. Understanding these physical experiences as echoes of past trauma can guide you towards comprehensive treatments that address both mind and body.

As you identify these signs, it's important to treat yourself with compassion and patience. Childhood traumas are complex and multifaceted. Emotional reactions such as anxiety, depression, and anger are more than passing feelings; they can be ingrained responses to prior experiences. Behavioral issues like substance abuse and self-sabotage, while counterproductive, are survival strategies. Difficulties in relationships, including trust issues and fear of connectedness, highlight the difficulties of forming secure bonds when early relationships were unstable. The physical symptoms remind you that your body can hold memories, often conveying what your mind hasn't yet processed.

Journaling About Traumatic Experiences

Journaling serves as a powerful means for grappling with childhood trauma, providing a safe environment to process and comprehend your deepest emotions. Start by creating a cozy space that encourages openness in your journaling practice. Choose a quiet spot where you feel secure and undisturbed. Personalizing this space with elements like soft lighting, pleasing scents, or calming music can enhance your experience. Establishing a routine signals to your mind and body that it's time to reflect and write.

Once your environment is set, explore various techniques to guide your thoughts. Stream-of-consciousness writing is a valuable method where you freely express your ideas, letting them flow without concern for structure. This approach can uncover hidden feelings and provide a sense of release. Alternatively, using prompts can be an effective strategy. These can be questions or statements that ignite self-reflection, such as "What emotional needs from my childhood went unmet?" or "Recall a challenging memory from my past and its impact on my life today." Such prompts lead you toward a deeper understanding of your experiences.

Letter writing offers another therapeutic option. You might write letters to different facets of yourself—your inner child, your present self, or even your future self—articulating thoughts and emotions that may be hard to express. Similarly, drafting letters to individuals who significantly impacted your trauma, regardless of whether you send them, can be profoundly healing. This practice allows you to voice your repressed feelings and provides a pathway toward closure.

Patience is essential on this journey. There is no prescribed pace or volume for your journaling. Each person's journey is unique and unfolds organically. Don't feel pressured to write perfectly or uncover profound insights during every session. It's perfectly acceptable to have entries that may seem trivial or unfinished; the crucial part is maintaining a compassionate approach and recognizing that some days, words will come easily while on others, they might not.

Reviewing your journal entries can reveal valuable insights into recurring themes and patterns. Dedicate time periodically to reflect on your past writings. Look for trends in your emotions, reactions, and lived experiences. You may observe similarities in your responses to specific triggers or fluctuations in your mood regarding certain memories. Spotting these patterns helps identify unresolved issues that may need more attention.

Besides evaluating content, notice how your writing style evolves. Do you express yourself more openly? Are there changes in your tone or vocabulary that indicate emotional progress? Recognizing these shifts can be encouraging, serving as a testament to the growth you've achieved through journaling.

Creating a regular journaling schedule is crucial for making the practice effective. Choose a time and place that fits into your routine, whether that's in the morning as you start your day or at night for reflection before sleep. Consistency fosters habit and deepens your engagement with thoughts and feelings.

The WRITE method (Adams, n.d.) offers a structured way to enhance your journaling sessions. First, identify what topic you want to explore. Next, take a moment to reflect on it, perhaps by closing your eyes and taking deep breaths to center yourself. Write continuously for a set time—between five to fifteen minutes—allowing thoughts and feelings to flow as they come . Conclude by reviewing what you've written, summarizing your insights in a sentence or two.

While journaling can sometimes unearth difficult emotions, remember this is a natural part of healing. Give yourself permission to fully experience these feelings without judgment. Your journal is a judgment-free zone where you can express anything openly. This freedom can be immensely liberating, allowing you to confront and work through challenging memories constructively.

Integrating mindfulness into your journaling ritual can further enrich its benefits. Mindfulness means being fully present and engaged in your current experience. Before you begin writing, take a moment to ground yourself. Pay attention to your breath, feel your physical body, and focus on the present. Starting your journaling session with this mindful awareness enhances your connection to your inner experiences.

Keep in mind that journaling is a flexible practice. There's no need to stick to one approach; feel free to switch techniques based on what resonates with you at the moment. Some days, you may prefer free writing, while on others, prompts or letter writing may feel more beneficial. This adaptability helps you stay engaged, customizing the process to fit your evolving needs.

Finally, sharing your journaling experiences with someone you trust—or with a therapist—can provide added layers of support. Discussing your insights can offer fresh perspectives and reinforce what you've learned. It fosters a sense of connection, reminding you that you're not alone on your healing journey.

> Meet Emma, a remarkable young woman who has always been known as the epitome of strength in her community. Yet beneath her vibrant surface lay the effects of past trauma. Growing up in a chaotic household filled with uncertainty, Emma often felt it necessary to suppress her emotions for survival. As an adult, this unresolved trauma manifested in chronic migraines that would strike unexpectedly, incapacitating her for days.

Emma's life took a significant turn when a particularly severe migraine pushed her to seek professional help. In therapy, she began connecting her emotional struggles—the sadness rooted in her childhood, the anxiety from a lack of safety—with the physical pain she experienced. With her therapist's guidance, she realized that her migraines weren't just physical but signs of unresolved emotional turmoil.

Through therapy, Emma unearthed mindfulness techniques and started journaling about her emotions, finally giving voice to feelings she had long suppressed. With dedication and time, she learned to manage her migraines and embarked on a profound self-discovery journey leading to significant healing.

Emma found inspiration as she shared her story at a local mental health event. Speaking about overcoming her emotional and physical challenges filled her with empowerment. Moved by her own journey, Emma became an advocate for others facing similar struggles, urging them to embrace their pain while seeking solutions.

> Emma's life is a compelling reminder that comprehending and addressing the manifestations of trauma is crucial for holistic healing. It highlights that the path to recovery may be long and arduous, yet it can also foster personal growth and inspire others along the way.

You can also heal from your past and support your inner self. You can become a source of hope and inspiration for others who are dealing with similar struggles. This book will give you the tools to achieve that.

Summary and Reflections

Understanding and recognizing past traumas is an important part of healing. When you think about different types of childhood trauma, like abuse, neglect, and abandonment, you begin to notice how these experiences link to your current feelings or behaviors. This awareness can help you break free from harmful patterns that might have lasted for years. It also opens the door to healthier relationships, greater emotional stability, and a more empowered life. In the next chapter, we will explore emotional awareness further and learn how to understand and express our feelings effectively.

Embracing Emotional Awareness

> "We cannot tell what may happen to us in the strange medley of life. But we can decide what happens in us — how we can take it, what we do with it — and that is what really counts in the end. " — Joseph Fort Newton

Emotional awareness means fully embracing your feelings and recognizing how they shape your experiences. It's not just about noticing your emotions; it's about understanding why you feel that way and what those feelings are trying to tell you. Just as a check engine light alerts you to a problem in your car, your emotions guide you through your mental and emotional landscape. For example, feeling low might signal your need for connection or comfort, while a burst of joy often reflects your alignment with what truly matters to you. By paying attention to these emotional cues, you create an opportunity for deep self-discovery and healing.

The Significance of Emotional Awareness

Emotional awareness plays a vital role in shaping our relationships. Recognizing and managing our emotions directly influences how we interact with others. When you're in tune with your feelings, you communicate more effectively, resolve conflicts with compassion, and build deeper connections.

Picture this: your best friend cancels plans at the last minute. It's natural to feel upset. So what do you do? Lash out in anger, give her the cold shoulder the next time you meet, or worry yourself thinking that she doesn't care for you anymore?

Instead of reacting in anger, take a moment to breathe and accept your disappointment. By identifying that 'I am feeling disappointed', you can share your thoughts in a positive way. Engaging in an open-hearted conversation about your feelings—rather than placing blame—can clear misunderstandings and strengthen your friendship.

Emotional awareness also underpins resilience. Being resilient isn't just about bouncing back; it involves understanding your emotional state to tackle life's challenges more efficiently. When you grasp your feelings, you're better equipped to create effective coping strategies.

Emotional awareness is the first step in the journey toward healing. Recognizing and processing your true emotions can pave the way for personal recovery, especially for those who've experienced trauma or emotional neglect. Unresolved feelings often resurface in current behaviors and thought patterns, hindering progress. By identifying and working through these emotions, you can start to break down the barriers you've built around your heart, kickstarting the healing process.

Understanding the difference between emotions and feelings is essential. Dr. Antonio Damasio describes emotions (Mari, 2017) as instinctual responses to stimuli, while feelings denote our conscious interpretations of those emotions. For example, before speaking in public, you might sense your heart racing and your palms sweating (emotions) and label that as anxiety or excitement (feelings). Recognizing this distinction makes it easier to navigate complex emotional experiences.

Developing emotional awareness isn't an overnight achievement; it takes ongoing practice and reflection. Mindfulness exercises can greatly enhance this awareness. Being mindful allows you to stay present, so you can observe your emotions objectively. When faced with challenges, taking a moment to breathe deeply and focus on the present can clarify your feelings and calm your mind (*Emotional Awareness: Definition, Benefits & Techniques* , n.d.). Another effective tool is emotional journaling; regularly documenting your feelings and their triggers reveals patterns and deepens your insight into your emotional world.

It's also useful to take a step back for self-reflection when you feel a strong emotion. Ask yourself what you're feeling and how it's influencing you. This practice can enhance your understanding of your emotional responses and promote greater emotional awareness.

Mindfulness-based therapies help people become aware of their emotions. They teach individuals to notice their feelings without getting too caught up in them, which helps improve emotional control and mental health.

Integrating emotional awareness into your daily life can amplify this skill. Activities like meditation, creative pursuits, and engaging with emotionally rich content such as books or films can deepen your understanding of both your own emotions and those of others. For instance, reading a novel that explores complex emotional themes can offer new perspectives and enhance your empathy, helping you connect more meaningfully with others.

Let's look at some relatable situations to understand emotional awareness. Imagine you're feeling stressed at work, your stomach tightens, and your heart races. Rather than pretending to be calm, admit to yourself that you're feeling overwhelmed. Taking a few mindful breaths can help you regain focus and approach your tasks with refreshed clarity.

Now, consider your personal relationships. If you notice your best friend acting unusually distant, it's natural to worry. Instead of jumping to conclusions or expressing frustration, acknowledge your concern about possibly losing this important connection. An open and honest conversation about your feelings—as opposed to blaming—can clear up misunderstandings and strengthen your relationship.

For those dealing with relationship challenges due to unprocessed emotions, this approach can be especially effective. By fostering emotional intelligence and recognizing your triggers, navigating conflicts becomes easier and enhances relationship dynamics. Couples who often find themselves in disputes may benefit from emotional awareness exercises that uncover the root causes of their conflicts, whether they relate to past traumas or current stressors.

> Meet Tom and Rachel, a married couple who had been together for nearly a decade. On the surface, they seemed like a happy family, raising two children and sharing a comfortable life. However, beneath the facade, both were grappling with unprocessed emotions from their past that began to create fissures in their relationship.
>
> Tom had experienced a tumultuous childhood with a father who was emotionally and sometimes physically abusive. Even though he had built a successful career and a loving family, the unresolved pain from his past haunted him, causing him to struggle with vulnerability and intimacy. Rachel, on the other hand, had grown up in a family that emphasized high achievement and perfectionism, leading her to develop an internal dialogue that constantly critiqued herself. This made her anxious about their relationship, as she feared she would never be good enough for Tom.
>
> Over time, the weight of their unprocessed

emotions began to affect their communication. Tom would often withdraw during conflicts, becoming increasingly silent and unreachable, which left Rachel feeling abandoned and frustrated. In turn, Rachel's anxiety would manifest as criticism and nagging, which Tom perceived as an attack, causing him to retreat further.

One evening, after a particularly heated argument about household responsibilities, a breakthrough moment occurred. Rachel, feeling vulnerable, decided to share her feelings openly for the first time. She spoke about her fears of inadequacy and how it made her react with frustration. In that moment, Tom realized that Rachel's words were not a reflection on him, but rather her own insecurities.

Touched by her honesty, Tom responded with surprising openness. He revealed his own struggles with vulnerability and how his childhood had made it difficult for him to communicate effectively. As they opened up to each other, both began to recognize how their past experiences influenced their reactions in their marriage.

That night marked a turning point. They agreed to prioritize open communication, even when it felt uncomfortable. They began to explore couples therapy, where they learned to unpack their unprocessed emotions together, transforming their relationship into a safe space for vulnerability.

Over time, Tom and Rachel found themselves growing closer, learning to express their insecurities and understanding each other's emotional landscapes. The journey wasn't easy, but by addressing their unprocessed emotions, they revitalized their relationship and strengthened the bond they had once thought was fading. Their experience shows that confronting emotional challenges together can lead to deeper intimacy and a more resilient partnership.

Strategies for Unearthing Suppressed Emotions

Identifying your suppressed emotions is an important step toward becoming more emotionally aware. Often, these hidden feelings sit beneath the surface, subtly shaping how you behave and feel overall.

Self-reflection can be a powerful tool for uncovering these buried emotions. Journaling is especially effective, as it allows you to express your thoughts and feelings freely. By setting aside a few minutes each day to write about your experiences, you create a safe environment for deeper understanding. Start with questions like, "What emotions did I feel today?" or "What situations made me uncomfortable?" Reflecting on these prompts can help you bring to light emotions that were previously hidden. Similarly, meditation promotes mindfulness, allowing you to observe your emotions without judgment.

Your body often gives clues about your emotional state. Physical symptoms can reflect feelings we're not fully aware of. Signs of suppressed emotions might show up as tension in your shoulders, frequent headaches, stomach problems, or fatigue. Noticing these physical signals can help you understand what emotions need your attention. For instance, a persistent headache at work might indicate stress or anxiety about your job. Body scans—where you mentally check in with each part of your body—can help uncover discomfort linked to specific emotions. Keeping a journal of these sensations and their corresponding feelings can create a clearer picture of your emotional state.

Engaging with your dreams can reveal more about your suppressed feelings. Dreams often act as reflections of our subconscious, highlighting emotions and conflicts that we might overlook in waking life. Keep a dream journal by your bed to quickly record your dreams upon waking. Look for themes and symbols, and consider what they might indicate about your emotional health. Are there hidden worries, aspirations, or unresolved conflicts appearing in your dreams? Exploring these insights can help you better understand emotions that might otherwise remain hidden. Over time, you may notice patterns that provide valuable insights into your inner self (McGowan, 2023).

Creative expression is another powerful way to process and communicate your hidden feelings. Activities like painting, writing, making music, or dancing offer unique outlets to express and understand your emotions. Art allows feelings to emerge without the constraints of words. If painting attracts you, let your brush explore the canvas using colors that reflect your current mood. Writing stories or poems can be therapeutic too, allowing you to channel emotions through characters. If you prefer movement, dance can serve as both an emotional and physical release. Embrace these creative methods as opportunities to dive into and express your repressed emotions in a supportive environment (Melany, 2020).

Practicing Mindfulness to Maintain Emotional Presence

Mindfulness is a powerful way to stay emotionally present and effectively process your feelings as they come up. By incorporating mindfulness into your everyday life, you can learn to manage your emotions skillfully, fostering a sense of calm and resilience within yourself.

Understanding Mindfulness

Mindfulness revolves around fully attending to the present moment without judgment. It's about noticing thoughts, feelings, and sensations as they are, rather than trying to alter or escape them. This practice enables individuals to authentically experience their emotions and understand their root causes. Essentially, mindfulness invites us to be completely present in our lives, allowing for easier management of stress and emotional challenges.

Breathing Techniques

One of the most effective approaches to cultivating mindfulness is through intentional breathing exercises. These practices anchor your emotions by directing your focus to the rhythm and sensations of your breath.

A simple yet powerful technique is the 4-7-8 breathing method. Start by inhaling deeply through your nose for a count of four, then hold that breath for seven counts before exhaling fully through your mouth for eight counts. Repeat this cycle several times. This practice not only gives you a clear focal point but also helps to lower your heart rate, promoting a state of relaxation and tranquility.

Another beneficial technique is belly breathing. Find a comfortable seated or lying position, placing one hand on your chest and the other on your stomach. Breathe in deeply through your nose, allowing your stomach to expand while keeping your chest still. As you exhale through your mouth, feel your stomach gently contract. By practicing this technique for a few minutes each day, you can significantly ease anxiety and enhance your emotional resilience.

Mindful Observation

Mindful observation consists of monitoring your thoughts and feelings without becoming attached. This technique encourages you to witness your emotions as they emerge, acknowledging them without judgment. Picture your emotions as leaves drifting on a stream—temporary and ever-evolving.

Begin by finding a quiet space free from distractions. Close your eyes and take a few deep breaths to center yourself. Then, simply observe any thoughts or feelings that arise. Instead of engaging with them, let them pass by like clouds across the sky. If you find yourself feeling overwhelmed, gently redirect your focus back to your breath.

This practice can be particularly useful during times of intense emotions. For example, when experiencing anger or frustration, taking a moment to observe those feelings can prevent rash reactions. Over time, mindful observation nurtures a deeper understanding of your emotional patterns, making it easier to respond thoughtfully to triggers.

Integrating Mindfulness into Daily Life

To maintain mindfulness throughout your day, incorporate simple, intentional practices into your routine. Here are some practical suggestions:

1. **Morning Routine** : Begin your day with a brief mindfulness session. Devote a few minutes to focus on your breath or engage in a body scan meditation, systematically paying attention to different parts of your body.
2. **Mindful Eating** : Transform mealtimes into chances for mindfulness. Notice the colors, textures, and flavors of your food. Chew deliberately and savor each bite, fully immersing yourself in the experience.
3. **Mindful Walking** : Infuse mindfulness into your walking by concentrating on the sensations of each step, the ground beneath your feet, and your body's movement. Take

note of the sounds, sights, and smells around you without hurrying to your destination.

4. **Mindfulness Breaks** : Throughout your day, take short breaks to practice mindfulness. Use these moments to check in with your emotional state and physical sensations. A few deep breaths or a brief pause can reset your mind and alleviate stress.
5. **Evening Reflection:** Conclude your day with a mindful reflection. Spend a few minutes revisiting your day, recognizing any emotions that surfaced and how you responded. This reflection can enhance self-awareness and ready your mind for restful sleep.

Beyond these practices, integrating mindfulness into daily tasks—like brushing your teeth, washing dishes, or folding laundry—can enrich your emotional well-being. The essence is to bring your full attention to whatever you're doing, allowing you to be engaged in each moment.

By incorporating mindfulness into various aspects of your daily life, you establish resilience against stress and promote a more harmonious emotional state. Give it a try; you might be surprised by the profound effects these seemingly simple practices like reflective journaling and mindfulness have on your emotional wellness.

Closing Thoughts

Recognizing your emotions as valuable guides to your inner world can help you navigate relationships and handle life's challenges with more empathy and resilience. By becoming more aware of your feelings, you can communicate more clearly, manage stress proactively, and build deeper connections with others. Laying this groundwork of emotional awareness is crucial for your personal healing, allowing you to confront past traumas and improve your mental well-being.

Moreover, we delved into effective techniques to enhance emotional awareness, such as practicing mindfulness and keeping an emotional journal. As you begin this journey, remember that developing emotional awareness takes time, patience, and commitment. With regular practice, you can build a strong emotional foundation that supports your healing and personal development.

Soon, you'll discover how to reconnect with your inner child through various therapeutic methods that promote healing and emotional growth.

Healing Practices and Techniques

> "To heal is to touch with love that which we previously touched with fear." – Stephen Levine

Healing your wounded inner child can be a transformative journey, bringing profound emotional relief and self-connection.

In this chapter, you will discover various therapeutic techniques aimed at fostering a deep connection between your current self and your inner child. Each method is designed to address the lingering impact of childhood trauma and empower you on your journey toward emotional recovery and self-compassion.

Guided Visualizations and Meditations

Creating a supportive space for your inner child through visualization and meditation can be a transformative journey toward deep emotional healing. By using these techniques, you can cultivate a safe environment for your wounded inner child, affirm feelings, and nurture self-love.

Guided visualizations are a powerful way to forge a comforting space for making this connection. Picture a sanctuary where your inner child feels entirely secure—this may be a sunny garden, a tranquil beach, or any comforting backdrop that resonates with you. As you immerse yourself in this visualization, invite your inner child to join you. This interaction fosters a feeling of emotional safety, helping your inner child gain the confidence to express itself. For instance, imagining yourself as a child enjoying a warm summer day at a fair can help you reconnect with joyful childhood moments. Crafting a peaceful mental landscape like this allows the sensitive parts of you to share emotions and start healing.

Meditation deepens this bond by facilitating conversations between your adult self and your inner child. These exchanges encourage acceptance and acknowledgment of the child's feelings. One helpful method is to sit quietly, focus on your breath, and gently direct your awareness toward your inner child. Ask questions like, "What do you need right now?" or "How can I provide support?”

Patience and active listening will allow you to get insights about unresolved past emotions. Gradually, this practice nurtures a sustained relationship between your adult self and your inner child, encouraging continual emotional healing.

Healing light visualizations are another excellent technique you can use. For this, envision a warm, healing light surrounding your body, with special attention on your inner child. Imagine this light as a loving energy of any color that resonates with you, filling every part of you, providing comfort and compassion. You can also visualize a radiant glow embracing and illuminating your inner child with warmth, helping you foster feelings of love, safety, and acceptance. If you like, you can put on some healing meditative music in the background while you practice this technique. Sending love and healing energy like this can significantly boost your sense of self-love and compassion, enhancing your self-image.

Integrating breathing techniques during your visualization and meditation sessions can make them even more effective. They connect your mind and body, keep you grounded in the present moment and reduce anxiety. Techniques like the "Simple Breath" exercise recommended by inner child healing therapist Robert Jackman involve slow, deliberate breaths that facilitate a state of calm. Breathing exercises, such as diaphragmatic breathing or synchronized rhythms, promote relaxation and concentration.

Begin by finding a quiet space free from distractions. Sit comfortably, resting one hand on your stomach. Inhale deeply through your nose, feeling your stomach expand, then exhale gently through your mouth as your stomach contracts. This mindful breathing can soothe your nervous system, alleviate stress, and create a favorable atmosphere for holistic emotional healing. Practicing these breathing techniques regularly not only aids relaxation but also strengthens your connection with your inner child, amplifying the overall impact of your healing journey.

The strength of these methods lies in their ability to address emotional wounds rooted in childhood experiences. For many individuals who have faced childhood trauma, feelings of neglect, abandonment, or rejection create deep psychological scars. Such wounds can shape how you perceive yourself and interact with others. Practical approaches like visualization and meditation provide pathways to revisit and heal these emotional injuries. Creating a secure mental environment allows your inner child to feel acknowledged and validated, a crucial step for emotional recovery (Raypole, 2020).

Recognizing and accepting your inner child's feelings through meditation can greatly improve your emotional health. When children grow up without enough emotional support, they might carry feelings of worthlessness or fear into adulthood. Meditation helps you pay attention to your thoughts and feelings, teaching you to acknowledge and accept them without judgment. This awareness makes it easier to notice and deal with triggers that cause negative reactions. By regularly sitting with and validating these feelings, you let your inner child know that it's okay to have and share emotions openly.

Incorporating these practices into daily life leads to small but important changes. Regularly practicing visualization, meditation, and breathing exercises creates a routine of caring for yourself, helping with emotional healing. Over time, you will start to see better control over your emotions, more self-acceptance, and improved relationships. This is especially important if you are grappling with unresolved emotional trauma as it gives you a simple structured approach to healing your emotional wounds and building healthier relationships.

Healing Through Creative Expression

Engaging in creative pursuits like art and music can be incredibly powerful for expressing emotions and promoting healing—especially if you're trying to reconnect with your inner child. These creative outlets grant you the ability to voice feelings that might be hard to express in words. By immersing yourself in art and music, you can enhance your emotional health and cultivate a deeper relationship with yourself.

Art therapy presents a wonderful opportunity to articulate emotions tied to your childhood experiences. Often, painful memories from your early years are buried within, lacking verbal representation. When words aren't sufficient, creating art can serve as a powerful means to release these hidden feelings. Activities like drawing, painting, or sculpting allow you to externalize your innermost thoughts, creating a tangible outlet for your emotions. This process encourages emotional release, providing a grounding and healing experience. The liberating environment of art allows you to explore your feelings freely, helping to dismantle emotional barriers and promoting a sense of relief and understanding (Great Valley Publishing Company, Inc, 2011).

Doing this in a nurturing environment—like a therapy group or among friends— amplifies these benefits. Research by Cumming and Visser (2009) indicates that being surrounded by supportive peers can uplift your confidence and self-worth. Sharing your creations in a trusting atmosphere counters feelings of isolation and shame often linked to childhood trauma. You may discover symbols and methods of expression that resonate with your experiences, ultimately building a sense of community and shared understanding.

Music and sound healing are vital for emotional expression and recovery as well. Music can trigger intense memories and feelings, serving as a connection to your past. The rhythms and melodies of certain songs can soothe and deepen your emotional resonance. For example, listening to music that held significance during your childhood can revive feelings tied to specific moments, allowing for emotional reflection and release. Sound healing methods, like drumming or using singing bowls, can help you relax and reduce stress.(Expressive Arts Therapy | Psychology Today, n.d.).

Integrating art and journaling can further enrich your emotional exploration. Expressing your thoughts visually through art and writing allows for a multi-faceted approach to self-discovery. Creating visual representations can reveal subconscious emotions, while journaling about the artwork helps clarify and analyze these insights. Keeping an art journal where you sketch or paint your emotions while reflecting on their meanings can uncover suppressed feelings and provide clarity about your emotional state.

Engaging in whimsical play with art and music is another effective healing strategy. This form of creativity fosters spontaneity, joy, and freedom, all of which may be stifled by unresolved childhood trauma. Activities like spontaneous drawing or composing playful songs enable you to reconnect with your inner child. Such creative play dismantles rigid emotional walls, allowing for sincere and uninhibited self-expression. Infusing therapy with a playful spirit makes the healing journey more enjoyable and less intimidating.

When using art therapy, it's crucial to approach your creations without self-judgment. Concentrate on the creative journey rather than the final product. This shift in perspective removes pressure and nurtures a safe environment for emotional exploration. A therapist or facilitator can direct you to explore diverse art materials and techniques, encouraging you to experiment and discover yourself. You can even use creative prompts, such as "illustrate a place where you feel secure" or "design an image that reflects your happiest memory."

When it comes to music and sound healing, selecting emotionally resonant pieces is key. You should feel encouraged to choose music that evokes strong feelings or memories, allowing for deeper engagement with your emotions. Therapists may incorporate guided imagery or meditation practices while listening to music, helping you visualize and process your experiences methodically. Group activities like community drumming or collective singing can enhance the feeling of support and connection, reinforcing the collective healing process.

Combining art and journaling can be particularly effective with a structured approach. A therapist might invite you to create an artwork and then spend time reflecting on it through writing. Prompts like "What emotions stirred within you while creating this?" or "How does this piece connect to your childhood?" can guide your journaling process. This technique fosters thorough exploration of emotions, aiding the understanding and release of complex feelings.

Expressive play with art and music should be approached with an open heart and flexible mindset. You should feel free to experiment with various mediums and activities, following your instincts and interests. Facilitators can introduce playful exercises, like collaborative painting or musical games, to ignite creativity and enhance interaction. It's important to keep an atmosphere of fun and curiosity, allowing you to shed inhibitions and reconnect with your inner child.

> One of the most transformative cases of inner child healing I've witnessed is Megan, a woman in her thirties who carried the heavy burden of childhood sexual abuse. Megan grew up in a home where the abuse was swept under the rug, leaving her with deep feelings of shame, helplessness, and isolation. For years, she suppressed these emotions, believing that silence was her only way to cope. As an adult, Megan struggled with low self-esteem, anxiety, and a pervasive sense of unworthiness, unable to fully connect with others or trust herself.
>
> When Megan began therapy, it became clear

that traditional methods alone weren't enough to help her access the deep, unspoken pain of her past. I suggested she try art therapy as a way to express the emotions she had buried for so long. Although hesitant at first, Megan soon found that creative expression became her voice when words failed. Through painting and drawing, she began to bring her inner child's pain to the surface. The colors, shapes, and imagery allowed her to express her anger, sadness, and shame in ways she had never been able to articulate.

As Megan poured her emotions into her artwork, a profound shift began to take place. She painted the darkness she had carried for so long, but also the light she longed to feel. Through her art, she began to confront the abuse that had left her feeling powerless and reclaim the parts of herself that had been lost. She realized that her inner child, once silenced by fear, could now speak through the brushstrokes and colors. It was through this process that Megan began to dismantle the deep-rooted shame she had lived with for years.

Over time, Megan started to use art not only to express her pain but to nurture her inner child. She painted images of safety and protection, giving her younger self the love and care she had never received. As she created these visual expressions, Megan's sense of self-worth grew. She learned that the abuse she endured didn't define her and that she had the power to create her own narrative. Art became a tool for empowerment, helping her reclaim her identity and release the shame she had carried for so long.

Megan's journey through creative expression was nothing short of remarkable. As she healed her inner child, she also began to overcome the feelings of helplessness that had once controlled her life. She developed healthier relationships, established boundaries, and found the confidence to trust herself again. Through the transformative power of art therapy, Megan not only healed the wounds of her past but discovered a sense of freedom and strength she never thought possible.

Therapeutic Journaling Prompts & Role-playing Exercises

Reflecting on your childhood and taking care of your inner child is important. One effective way to do this is through journaling. Writing about your past helps you discover feelings you may not have understood before and can lead to positive change through understanding and kindness towards yourself.

Reflective journaling helps you remember forgotten parts of your past, allowing you to examine them more closely. Try setting aside quiet time each day to write about your childhood memories. Use questions like "Describe your childhood in one sentence" or "What traits from your childhood do you still have?" As you write, you may uncover feelings and patterns that you didn't notice before. This process not only looks at your past, but it also helps you see how those memories affect your current feelings and actions. By approaching these memories with kindness and compassion, you can recognize past pains and begin to heal.

Writing letters to your inner child is an important journaling activity. This practice helps you express your feelings, offer comfort, and understand emotions that might have been overlooked. Begin by writing a letter to your younger self, giving love and support. Talk about the happy moments, the struggles, and the fears you experienced back then. These letters create a connection between your adult self and your younger self, healing wounds from the past. It's a caring way to show your inner child that their feelings matter and are acknowledged.

By using journaling prompts to explore your current feelings and wishes, you can uncover what you might have been ignoring and highlight the need to address emotional needs for your own healing. Questions like "What would you change about your childhood?" or "What activities made you happy as a child?" can help you find parts of your life that need care today. These questions encourage you to think about what your younger self wanted but didn't get—like love, safety, or freedom. Recognizing these unmet needs allows you to take the steps necessary for your healing journey, shifting your attention from just thinking about past events to actively seeking the emotional satisfaction you've been missing.

Role-playing exercises can help you set healthy boundaries, find support, and practice being kind to yourself. When you do guided role-play, you can recreate moments from your past when you felt weak or unsupported. For example, think about a time when a parent ignored your feelings as a child. In this scenario, let your adult self speak up for your inner child's needs. Clearly express your feelings and create boundaries that were missing in your childhood. This practice shows that you deserve respect and understanding from others and from yourself.

Another helpful role-playing activity is to imagine supportive people in your life. Picture or act out moments where caring characters—whether real or made up—bring you comfort and guidance. This could be a wise figure, a kind friend, or a loving version of yourself. By doing these positive exercises, you can replace bad memories from your childhood with good ones, helping your inner child feel safe and secure. Regularly practicing these interactions builds a strong sense of care and support, which is essential for emotional healing.

Engaging in self-compassion through role-play means treating your inner child's pain with kindness. If a memory brings up feelings of guilt or shame, take a moment to talk to your inner child. Speak kindly to them, as you would to a good friend. Let them know it's okay to feel hurt and that they are not at fault for what happened. This practice helps you learn to forgive yourself, which is important for healing.

Keeping a regular journaling practice is also important. You don't have to write on a strict schedule; you can write daily, weekly, or whenever you feel like connecting with yourself. The main points are to be consistent and intentional. Find a quiet place where you won't be interrupted. When you write, do it with an open heart and a sense of understanding. Over time, this regular practice can strengthen your connection to your inner child and boost your self-awareness and emotional strength.

Healing from childhood trauma takes dedication, patience, and a willingness to face your feelings. Journaling and role-playing are helpful ways to explore these feelings. They allow you to reconnect with and take care of your inner child. These activities help you stop self-destructive patterns, build healthier relationships with yourself and others, and develop a deeper sense of self-compassion and understanding.

Final Thoughts

In this chapter, you learned different ways to heal your inner child. Through guided imagery, you made a safe mental space where your inner child feels secure and can express itself. Meditation helped you connect more deeply with yourself, allowing you to understand and accept your feelings. By imagining healing light, you felt warmth and kindness, boosting your self-love and positive self-image. Breathing techniques used in these activities helped you relax and concentrate, which are important for emotional healing.

As we conclude, remember that these techniques can help you face childhood challenges and support continuous emotional healing. By regularly practicing visualization, meditation, mindful breathing and journaling, you help your inner child and improve your emotional health. These routines create a strong link between your adult self and your inner child, leading to better self-acceptance and emotional balance. By using these methods regularly, you can heal past wounds and form healthier relationships in your daily life.

Next, we will look at the power of self-compassion and its important role in our journey toward emotional healing.

Cultivating Self-Compassion

> "It's not your job to like me - It's mine. " - Byron Katie

Cultivating self-compassion is a vital step in your healing journey. It means treating yourself with kindness and understanding, especially during tough times like failure or suffering. Many people unintentionally hinder their emotional strength and well-being by being overly critical of themselves. When you learn to show yourself the same compassion you would offer a struggling friend, you unlock the path to deep inner peace and recovery.

Understanding Self-Compassion and Its Benefits

Self-compassion means treating yourself with kindness and understanding, especially during difficult times. This idea, pioneered by Kristin Neff, revolves around three main principles: self-kindness, recognizing our shared humanity, and practicing mindfulness. Self-kindness involves offering warmth and support to yourself when things don't go as planned, rather than harshly judging yourself. Picture how you would comfort a friend: you deserve that same compassion.

Recognizing that suffering is a universal human experience is a vital aspect of self-compassion. Instead of feeling alone in your struggles, remember that everyone faces challenges. This awareness helps you connect with others and diminishes feelings of isolation. Mindfulness, the third principle, encourages you to acknowledge your painful emotions without being overwhelmed by them. By calmly observing your feelings, you prevent yourself from letting negative experiences define you and maintain emotional clarity.

Embracing self-compassion can greatly enhance your mental health, helping to alleviate anxiety and depression. Research indicates that when you cultivate self-compassion, you're less prone to persistent negative thoughts and more capable of handling stress. For instance, instead of berating yourself for a mistake at work, recognize what happened, learn from it, and move forward, leaving the feelings of inadequacy behind. This practice not only alleviates immediate discomfort but also strengthens your emotional resilience in the long run.

Different cultures have various interpretations and expressions of self-compassion, which can shape personal development. In many Eastern traditions, self-compassion is woven into daily life through practices like meditation and mindfulness. Buddhist teachings, for example, highlight self-kindness and compassion as essential to achieving inner peace. In contrast, Western cultures often emphasize individual achievement and self-criticism, which can obstruct the cultivation of self-compassion. Understanding these cultural distinctions can empower you to adopt self-compassionate practices that align with your personal values, enriching your growth.

Extensive research underscores the importance of self-compassion for emotional health, motivation, and resilience. A review by Crego et al. (2022) found that self-compassion correlates with numerous positive outcomes, including diminished burnout and enhanced well-being among mental health professionals. Their study showed that self-compassion training programs significantly improve emotional resilience and reduce occupational stress. This highlights the potential of self-compassion to nurture a more balanced and healthier mental state.

Further evidence from Rushforth et al. (2023) reveals similar benefits for healthcare workers, noting that self-compassion initiatives increased well-being and alleviated secondary traumatic stress symptoms (STS). This highlights the importance of incorporating self-compassion practices into your daily routine can protect against mental health challenges, promoting emotional stability.

The scientific community has also shown that self-compassion boosts motivation and resilience. When you're kind to yourself, you're more inclined to chase your goals, even when you face setbacks. This happens because self-compassion lessens your fear of failure and nurtures a growth mindset. Rather than viewing failures as reflections of your worth, you start to see them as valuable opportunities to learn and evolve. This shift empowers your persistence and leads to long-term success.

Additionally, self-compassion helps counteract negative self-talk, fostering a more positive outlook on your journey. Self-critical thoughts can significantly harm your self-esteem and motivation. However, by practicing self-compassion, you can replace these damaging thought patterns with supportive ones. For example, instead of telling yourself, "I always mess up," you could reframe it as, "Mistakes are part of being human; I can learn from this and improve next time." This adjustment promotes a healthier self-image and elevates your spirit.

Exercises to Foster Self-Kindness

Self-compassion is essential for your healing journey, and a simple method to nurture it is through guided meditation. Meditation helps you center your thoughts and emotions, creating room for acceptance and kindness towards yourself. Start by finding a quiet, comfortable spot where you won't be interrupted. Sit or lie down with your eyes closed, and turn your attention to your breath. Notice the gentle rise and fall of your chest with each inhale and exhale. As you breathe in, embrace who you are right now. With each exhale, visualize letting go of negativity and self-judgment.

Incorporating affirmations during meditation can amplify its benefits. As you breathe, silently say phrases like, "I deserve love and kindness," or "I accept myself as I am." These affirmations strengthen your self-worth. You might also place your hand over your heart as a comforting gesture, helping you to feel more grounded in self-care (Gupta, 2024).

Another effective exercise is writing a self-compassion letter. Set aside some time to compose a letter to yourself as if you were your own compassionate friend. Identify an aspect of yourself where you feel less than perfect or are facing challenges. Write with empathy, acknowledging your feelings and offering encouragement. Recognize your pain while reminding yourself that everyone has flaws and makes mistakes. Share words of support, just like you would for someone you deeply care about. Keep this letter handy to revisit during tough times, allowing it to remind you of your intrinsic value.

Recognizing and reframing negative self-talk is vital for building a compassionate mindset. Pay close attention to the critical thoughts that run through your mind. If you catch yourself thinking, "I'm not enough," take a moment to question that belief. Ask if it's true or if it stems from negative past experiences. Reframe it into a kinder statement, like, "I am doing my best, and that is sufficient."

Consider maintaining a journal specifically to track your negative thoughts and to jot down alternative compassionate responses. Over time, you will notice a change in how you view yourself, slowly replacing harsh criticism with gentle understanding.

Daily self-compassion rituals can greatly enhance your well-being. Simple actions, such as starting each day with affirmations or taking short breaks for mindfulness, can help cultivate a compassionate mindset. Every morning, take a few moments to look in the mirror and speak three affirmations aloud. Try statements like, "I am strong," "I deserve happiness," or "I trust myself." These affirmations set a positive foundation for your day.

Prioritizing small acts of self-care in your daily routine is equally important. This could be as easy as engaging in enjoyable activities like reading a book, enjoying a bubble bath, or strolling through nature. These small gestures remind you that your well-being is valuable and worthy of attention.

Additionally, create a calming bedtime routine to encourage self-kindness. Before sleeping, take a few minutes to reflect on your day, recognizing both challenges and accomplishments without judgement. Engage in relaxing activities such as sipping herbal tea, practicing gentle yoga, or listening to soothing music. This not only prepares you for a restful night but also reinforces that you are worthy of care

By integrating these practical exercises into your daily life, you can gradually cultivate a kinder and more compassionate relationship with yourself. Guided meditations, self-compassion letters, reframing negative thoughts, and daily rituals all contribute to a holistic approach to emotional healing and resilience.

Keep in mind that developing self-compassion is a continuous journey, and it's perfectly fine to take it one step at a time. The key is to be consistent and patient with yourself. As these practices become second nature, you will find yourself feeling more grounded, resilient, and at peace with who you are.

Affirmations and Positive Self-Talk

The role of affirmations and positive self-talk in building self-compassion is vital. These approaches are essential for developing emotional strength and healing from past wounds. Affirmations are positive directives that reflect your core values and aspirations, influencing your mindset and beliefs. By actively practicing positive self-talk, you cultivate a mental space that enhances your overall well-being.

Crafting Personal Affirmations

To start creating personal affirmations, take some time to think about your experiences and what matters most to you. Your affirmations should connect with your core beliefs and goals. Identify specific areas in your life where you desire growth or support. For example, if you often doubt your self-worth, you could say, "I am worthy of love and respect." By personalizing your affirmations to reflect your own journey, you make them genuine and powerful.

When crafting your affirmations, focus on positivity, specificity, and, above all, use the present tense. Positive wording can shift negative thoughts into hopeful ones, while being specific clarifies what you truly desire. Using the present tense conveys that your goals are attainable right now, rather than in some uncertain future. Choose encouraging words that uplift and motivate you, turning each affirmation into a strong reminder of your inner strength.

Daily Affirmation Practices

Incorporating affirmations into your daily life is essential for their success. Choose specific times for this habit, such as during your morning routine or right before bedtime, to help you stay consistent. Starting your day with affirmations can empower you, reminding you of your worth and abilities as you tackle daily challenges. Meanwhile, affirmations at night can serve as a way to reflect, allowing you to close the day positively and nurture self-kindness.

Creating a special spot for your affirmation practice can boost its effectiveness. A serene corner with few distractions can help you concentrate and engage deeply with your words. Many find it beneficial to jot down their affirmations in a journal or place sticky notes around their home. These visual reminders keep your affirmations prominent in your mind, reinforcing their meaning throughout your day.

Transforming Negative Self-Talk

Negative self-talk often stems from long-held beliefs formed by past experiences. Fortunately, with mindful effort, you can turn these negative thoughts into uplifting affirmations. Start by noticing your internal dialogue—recognize when it shifts to negativity. Common thoughts might include "I'm not worthy" or "I always mess things up."

When you spot a negative thought, question its truth and substitute it with a kinder statement. Rather than telling yourself "I never succeed," consider saying "I have the ability to learn and grow from my experiences." This shift not only changes your immediate feelings but also gradually reforms your core beliefs over time. Consistently practicing this can turn your inner dialogue into a powerful source of encouragement and support.

Engaging with Supportive Networks

Engaging with supportive networks can greatly enhance your practice of positive self-talk and affirmations. When we surround ourselves with people who understand our journey, we build accountability and create a caring atmosphere.

Consider sharing your affirmations with trustworthy friends or joining groups dedicated to personal growth and healing.

These positive connections serve as a strong foundation for encouragement and shared wisdom. Listening to others' experiences can provide fresh insights that enrich your own journey. Moreover, articulating your affirmations in a group can amplify their significance, as speaking them aloud often makes them feel more tangible and achievable.

Support networks also promote consistency in your practice. Regular gatherings or check-ins can remind you to focus on affirmations and positive self-talk, making sure these practices stay integrated into your daily life. Within a group, the shared energy and dedication of everyone can really boost the effect of what you do on your own.

Practical Application

Integrating affirmations and positive self-talk into your daily routine means forming habits that nurture these practices. Dedicate a few minutes each day to focus on your affirmations. Make this a regular part of your day; the more consistently you practice, the stronger the benefits you'll experience.

Pairing affirmations with mindfulness can boost their impact. Before reciting your affirmations, take a moment to breathe deeply and ground yourself. This brief pause centers you in the present, helping you connect more fully with the empowering statements you're expressing. As you inhale deeply and repeat your affirmations, picture them coming to life in your mind. Visualize every detail vividly. This imagery strengthens your conviction that your aspirations are attainable.

Furthermore, approach this journey with kindness and patience toward yourself. Transforming long-held thought patterns requires time and dedication. Celebrate your small achievements and recognize the hard work you're investing in fostering self-compassion. Keep in mind that your focus should be on progress, not perfection.

> One of the most impactful cases of inner child healing I've worked on involved Sarah, a woman in her late thirties who carried deep emotional wounds from a childhood filled with harsh criticism and rejection. Growing up, Sarah's parents had impossibly high expectations, and no matter what she did, it was never enough. Mistakes were met

with harsh words, and affection was rare. As a result, Sarah developed a crippling fear of failure and a constant inner voice that told her she wasn't good enough.

By the time Sarah reached adulthood, this inner voice had become her constant companion. She was a high achiever, but no matter how much she accomplished, she always felt inadequate. She criticized herself for every mistake and struggled with overwhelming feelings of guilt and shame. Her inner child was still seeking the approval and love she had never received, but instead of finding kindness within herself, Sarah only reinforced the patterns of judgment she had grown up with.

When Sarah began therapy, we introduced the practice of self-compassion. At first, the concept was foreign to her—she had spent so many years criticizing herself that the idea of showing herself kindness felt uncomfortable. But as we worked together, Sarah began to understand that healing her inner child required treating herself with the same care she would offer a close friend or loved one.

Through guided self-compassion exercises, Sarah learned to soften the harsh inner critic that had controlled her for so long. When her inner child's voice would rise up with feelings of fear or inadequacy, instead of shutting it down, she started to respond with gentleness and understanding. She learned to say to herself, "It's okay to make mistakes. You are still worthy of love."

This shift in her thinking was transformative. Over time, Sarah began to experience a deep sense of relief. Her constant anxiety about not being good enough started to fade, replaced by a growing sense of self-acceptance. She no longer pushed herself to impossible standards or punished herself for every perceived failure. Instead, she embraced her imperfections and acknowledged her humanity.

As Sarah practiced self-compassion, her relationship with herself changed. She became more patient, more forgiving, and kinder to her inner child. The shame and guilt that had weighed her down for years began to lift, and she found a new sense of

> freedom and peace. In nurturing her inner child with compassion, Sarah healed the wounds of her past and discovered that the love she had been searching for was within her all along. Through this practice, she not only healed but also built a stronger, more resilient self, capable of facing life's challenges with grace and kindness.

Final Thoughts

Understanding and embracing self-compassion is a crucial milestone on your healing journey. By showing kindness to yourself, you can build emotional resilience and handle life's challenges more smoothly. In this chapter, you also learned about actionable techniques like guided meditations, writing letters to yourself filled with compassion, and shifting negative thoughts into more constructive patterns, all designed to foster a nurturing and forgiving mindset.

As you progress on your emotional healing journey, remember that patience and consistency are essential. By weaving these self-compassion practices into your everyday life, you can gradually reshape your inner voice to be more supportive and loving. Take small steps, treat yourself gently, and recognize the advancements you make along the way. Over time, you'll find that offering yourself compassion becomes as natural as breathing, guiding you towards a more serene and balanced state of being.

On the journey of understanding ourselves and gaining strength, it's important to see how setting and respecting boundaries can change our lives. In the next chapter, we will talk about ways to recognize when boundaries are crossed, helping you build emotional strength and form better relationships with others.

Setting Healthy Boundaries

> "Daring to set boundaries is about having the courage to love ourselves even when we risk disappointing others." – Brené Brown

Setting healthy boundaries is essential for emotional well-being and personal growth. Boundaries help us define our limits, express our needs, and protect our mental and emotional health. In a world where expectations often collide with personal needs, understanding how to establish and maintain these boundaries can significantly impact our quality of life and relationships.

Recognizing Boundary Violations

Understanding your personal boundaries is the crucial first step in noticing when they are being crossed and recognizing the effects on your emotional well-being. These boundaries can generally be divided into three primary types: physical, emotional, and time.

Physical boundaries define your comfort with personal space, touch, privacy, and sexual interactions. They help you understand the degree of closeness and contact you're comfortable with. For instance, while some individuals enjoy hugging friends, others may prefer a simple handshake or no physical interaction at all. Emotional boundaries focus on distinguishing your feelings and responsibilities from those of other people. This means owning your emotions without feeling pressured to manage or absorb the feelings of others. Time boundaries are about managing and valuing your time and energy. Recognizing when certain activities or obligations become overwhelming and knowing when to decline can significantly protect your well-being.

It's vital to recognize the signals that indicate your boundaries may have been breached. Common signs include discomfort, resentment, fatigue, or stress. If an individual's behavior leaves you feeling uneasy or if you often find yourself sacrificing your needs to please others, your boundaries could be in jeopardy. Overcommitting, feeling responsible for the happiness of those around you, or experiencing anxiety and irritation with specific people can also indicate boundary challenges.

Understanding the difference between healthy and unhealthy boundaries enhances your self-awareness. Healthy boundaries involve openly communicating your limits while respecting the boundaries of others. Examples of this include valuing your own boundaries, saying "no" without feeling guilty, and gracefully accepting when others decline. It also means sharing appropriately and maintaining a healthy give-and-take in relationships. Conversely, unhealthy boundaries demonstrate a lack of respect for personal limits and values, often allowing others to define your actions or self-worth. This may manifest in not saying "no" due to fear of rejection, feeling obligated to solve others' problems, or accepting unwanted physical touch or emotional demands.

Ignoring boundary violations can harm your emotional and mental health over time. When boundaries are crossed repeatedly, it can damage your self-esteem, trust, and sense of safety in relationships. This can lead to stress, resentment, and feeling worn out. You might also become dependent on others' approval, making your self-worth rely on what they think. This can cause you to ignore your own needs to seek praise from others, resulting in anxiety, depression, and trouble forming healthy relationships.

Knowing your personal boundaries is important for recognizing when they're crossed and understanding the effects of these violations. Being aware of boundary breaches can signal the need for changes to protect your personal space and emotional health. Understanding the difference between healthy and unhealthy boundaries helps you become more self-aware and encourages better relationships.

Steps to Assertively Communicate Boundaries

Effective boundary setting is essential for your emotional health and personal development. To help you communicate your boundaries with confidence and clarity, consider these practical strategies.

Using "I" Statements

A powerful method for assertively articulating your needs is through "I" statements. This approach enables you to share your feelings without sounding accusatory. For example, rather than saying, "You never listen to me," try saying, "I feel disregarded when you interrupt our conversations." This technique shifts the conversation to your emotions, increasing the likelihood that the other person will respond positively. By using "I" statements, you advocate for yourself while encouraging a more open response from others. Focus on what you need instead of pointing fingers or laying blame.

Timing and Environment

Selecting the right time and place to discuss boundaries is just as crucial. Addressing sensitive matters in a calm, private setting can significantly impact the outcome. Avoid broaching boundary topics in heated moments or public spaces where either of you may feel uncomfortable. Opt for a relaxed environment where open dialogue can thrive—such as discussing your need for personal space during a quiet evening rather than a tense family gathering. The right atmosphere can facilitate clearer communication and reduce misunderstandings.

Practice Active Listening

Engaging in active listening is fundamental when discussing boundaries. It's vital to pay attention to the other person's perspective as well, which demonstrates respect for their feelings and fosters mutual understanding. Show that you are listening by maintaining eye contact, nodding, and using verbal affirmations like "I understand" or "That makes sense." Additionally, paraphrase what you've heard to confirm your comprehension. For example, say, "So, you're feeling overwhelmed when I don't help with the household duties." Valuing the other person's input can encourage them to reciprocate your boundaries. Active listening nurtures a balanced conversation and lays the groundwork for respectful boundary-setting.

Follow Up to Clarify

After initiating boundary discussions, it's important to follow up to confirm mutual understanding. Revisit the conversation to strengthen your boundaries and clarify any potential confusion. Don't hesitate to bring up the topic again if your boundaries seem overlooked. A simple approach like, "I wanted to check in regarding our chat about [boundary] to ensure we're aligned," can help maintain clarity and reinforce respect. Following up ensures that your boundaries remain clear over time and allows space for any necessary adjustments.

Overcoming Guilt and Fear in Setting Boundaries

Establishing healthy boundaries is vital for your emotional well-being and personal development. Yet, navigating the path to set these limits can stir feelings of guilt and fear. To manage these emotions effectively, it's crucial to explore their roots, shift your mindset, take small steps toward bravery, and gather supportive friends around you.

Understanding where your guilt and fear come from often starts with examining the beliefs you've carried since childhood. Many of us grow up with the notion that prioritizing others' needs over our own is commendable. This mindset can create inner turmoil when trying to set boundaries, leading you to feel selfish or unkind. Moreover, societal and cultural expectations further complicate this. For example, women are often encouraged to take on roles as caregivers and peacekeepers, making boundary-setting feel uncomfortable or wrong, which can trigger guilt.

Fear arises from worries about what might happen if you establish boundaries. You might dread upsetting others, losing relationships, or being labeled as difficult. This fear can be immobilizing, making it hard to express your needs. Recognizing that these fears often stem from past experiences helps you view them as learned reactions, not absolute realities. By acknowledging the sources of your guilt and fear, you start to reduce their power over you.

A helpful approach to dealing with guilt and fear is to reframe your thoughts. This means transforming negative thinking into more positive or neutral perspectives. When guilt surfaces about setting a boundary, consider whether it's justified. Is it truly wrong to protect your well-being? Techniques like positive affirmations can be beneficial. For instance, if you're anxious about asserting a boundary at work, remind yourself that "My health and well-being matter. This boundary will enhance my job performance" (Lee, 2022). Shifting your perspective diminishes the strength of guilt and fear, empowering you to act in your best interest.

Taking incremental steps to cultivate courage is another essential strategy. Instead of attempting to overhaul all your boundaries at once, focus on minor changes first. Start by declining small requests that don't align with your priorities. Gradually work your way up to more significant boundaries. This approach helps you become desensitized to the fear surrounding boundary-setting, making it easier to tackle larger challenges. Each small victory builds your confidence and reinforces the idea that setting boundaries is both attainable and advantageous.

Surrounding yourself with supportive people can make setting boundaries easier. Connect with friends, family, coworkers, or support groups who understand and value personal boundaries. Watching others who confidently set their own boundaries can be a good example. It shows that having limits can improve relationships by building trust and respect. Additionally, having a supportive network offers encouragement and validation, making it easier to overcome feelings of guilt and fear (Lee, 2022).

Being part of a supportive community also brings practical advantages. By sharing your boundary-setting experiences with trusted allies, you can gain fresh insights and strategies for various situations. Practicing potential scenarios with supportive friends creates a safe space to refine your approach. This preparation boosts your confidence and lessens anxiety when facing real-life challenges.

Another effective technique is to visualize different perspectives. Think about how a caring friend would react to your situation. Would they advise you to disregard your own needs for others, or would they champion your right to self-care? This mindset helps create emotional distance, allowing you to view your circumstances more clearly. For instance, if a family member is trying to guilt you into compliance, consider the advice you would offer to a friend in a similar position. This practice can strengthen your determination and lessen the impact of guilt (Martin, 2021).

Reflecting on your experiences by writing in a journal can provide valuable insights. Writing about your feelings and the results of setting boundaries helps you understand your emotions and track your progress. Thinking through your actions helps you see what works and what needs improvement. This ongoing self-checking supports your personal growth and improves your ability to create and keep healthy boundaries.

Lily's journey illustrates how embracing boundaries can lead to a healthier, more fulfilling life.

Lily was my son's school teacher. She was unwaveringly devoted and consistently prioritized the needs of her students and colleagues above all else. She loved her job and genuinely wanted to help everyone around her, but over time, she began to feel overwhelmed and drained. Her evenings were consumed by lesson planning and grading, leaving little time for herself or her family.

Recognizing that her well-being was suffering, Lily decided it was time to set boundaries. She took a step back and assessed her commitments, realizing that she needed to prioritize her own needs to remain effective and joyful in her role as a teacher.

One of the first boundaries she established was a dedicated "no work" zone after 6 PM. She informed her colleagues and students that she would no longer respond to emails or take calls during the evening. This decision was tough at first, as she feared disappointing others, but she understood that maintaining her mental health was crucial.

Lily also started to prioritize her personal time by scheduling regular self-care activities, like yoga classes and book club meetings with friends. She communicated her needs to her family and colleagues, letting them know that taking this time for herself would help her be more present and effective in her teaching.

As a result of these boundaries, Lily experienced a remarkable transformation. She found herself with renewed energy and a clearer mindset, allowing her to engage more passionately with her students and enjoy her interactions with colleagues. Her relationships at work improved as she became more positive and less stressed, and she felt more connected to her family during their evenings together.

Lily's story shows how important it is to set boundaries in our lives. By prioritizing her own well-being, she not only enhanced her

> happiness but also fostered healthier, more meaningful relationships with others. Her journey inspires us to recognize that boundaries are not just limitations; they are essential tools that empower us to live fuller, happier lives while nurturing those we care about.

Concluding Thoughts

Boundaries are important for our emotional health and personal growth. They can be physical, emotional, or related to our time, and recognizing when these boundaries are crossed can help us manage feelings of discomfort and stress. When we understand our boundaries, we can take action to protect our needs and share our limits with others, which creates a safer and more respectful environment.

Setting healthy boundaries requires being aware of ourselves, communicating clearly, and sticking to our limits while also respecting others. This is a continuous process that takes patience and practice but leads to stronger and more balanced relationships. By learning to set boundaries, we can prevent issues like chronic stress and low self-esteem. Overall, recognizing and maintaining healthy boundaries is vital for our emotional well-being, improving our relationships, and supporting our personal development.

As we continue our exploration of personal growth, it's important to turn our attention to the dynamics of relationships and how our early experiences shape our connections with others. The next chapter will give you crucial insights and practical tools to enhance and heal your interpersonal relationships.

Improving Relationship Dynamics

> "A strong relationship requires choosing to love each other even in those moments when you struggle to like each other." - Dave Willis

Improving how you relate to others goes beyond merely recognizing your interactions; it means examining the deep-seated patterns that influence your actions and reactions. These patterns often root from childhood experiences, especially the initial bonds formed with your caregivers, which shape your attachment styles. Knowing about these influences and learning about different attachment styles can help you see how your past affects your current relationships and what you can do to improve them.

Understanding Attachment Styles

Understanding and improving how you connect with others is important for building solid, healthy relationships. One key idea to look at is attachment theory. This theory explains how your early life experiences shape how you relate to others. By knowing your own attachment style and that of your partner, you can create stronger emotional bonds and improve your relationships.

Attachment theory, pioneered by John Bowlby and Mary Ainsworth, illustrates how early interactions with caregivers influence your behavior in adult relationships. There are four main attachment styles: secure, anxious, avoidant, and disorganized. Secure attachment allows you to view yourself and others positively, fostering responsive and healthy relationships. Anxious attachment often leads to dependence and fears of abandonment, resulting in clingy behaviors. Avoidant attachment may express itself through emotional distance and difficulty forming close bonds. Disorganized attachment features inconsistent and confused behaviors, often a consequence of past trauma.

Identifying your attachment style is a vital step in understanding your relationship patterns. Begin by reflecting on your past relationships and your childhood experiences. Consider how you felt when separated from loved ones and how you reacted during reunions. For instance, if you experienced anxiety during separations and immense relief upon return, you may lean toward an anxious attachment style. Conversely, if you felt indifferent during these instances, this might suggest an avoidant style. Examining these patterns can enlighten your current behaviors and tendencies.

Additionally, reviewing your relationship history can provide clues about your attachment style. Look for recurring themes like fear of intimacy, dependency, or a tendency to withdraw. Recognizing these patterns enables you to communicate your needs more effectively and forge healthier connections. Remember, attachment styles exist along a spectrum, so you may not neatly fit into one category. However, identifying your predominant style can be empowering.

The effects of attachment on relationships are significant. Individuals with secure attachments generally experience easier, more trusting relationships. They balance intimacy and independence effectively. Conversely, those with anxious attachment may grapple with worries about their partner's commitment, leading to conflicts and misunderstandings. Those with avoidant attachment often prioritize independence, which can hinder closeness and meaningful connections. Disorganized attachment may result in erratic behaviors and difficulty maintaining stable relationships due to unresolved past traumas.

Your early experiences play a major role in shaping these attachment styles. Children who grow up with consistent, responsive caregivers learn to trust others and see themselves positively, developing secure attachments. In contrast, children with unpredictable or neglectful caregivers may develop insecure attachment styles. Anxiously attached children often cling to caregivers out of fear, while avoidant children may become emotionally distant and self-reliant. Disorganized attachment often stems from confusing caregiver behaviors, leaving children unsure of how to navigate their environments.

Understanding how early experiences affect adult relationships helps you break free from unhelpful patterns. Recognizing that these patterns come from past interactions allows you to approach relationships with more empathy and awareness. This understanding helps you be patient and compassionate with both yourself and your partner as you navigate your emotions together.

Changing to a secure attachment style is possible with effort and practice. It starts with being open and vulnerable. Being vulnerable means sharing your true feelings and fears without holding back. This can be risky, as it involves trusting that your partner will respond with care. Such openness can strengthen your connections and create a safe space for both of you to share your needs.

Good communication is essential for moving toward a secure attachment style. Work on expressing your feelings and needs clearly and respectfully. Use "I" statements to share your feelings without blaming your partner. For example, saying, “I feel unsupported when you aren’t available to talk,” encourages positive conversations and lowers defensiveness, leading to better understanding.

Building a secure attachment also means being emotionally present and available. Show genuine interest in your partner's feelings and experiences. Listening without judgment or interruption shows that you value their perspective, which builds trust and strengthens your bond.

In addition to open communication and emotional availability, being consistent is important for developing a secure attachment. Consistent actions build reliability and predictability, which are important for trust. Keeping your promises and being dependable reassures your partner that they can count on you, creating safety and security in your relationship.

Another helpful way to strengthen your attachment is by practicing gratitude. Regularly expressing appreciation for your partner and recognizing the good things in your relationship creates a supportive environment. Gratitude boosts positivity and strengthens your bond, highlighting the unique contributions of each person.

Keep in mind that moving to a secure attachment style takes time. Patience and determination are crucial as you work through old patterns and adopt new behaviors. If necessary, seek professional help. Therapy can provide useful tools and guidance to address underlying attachment issues and support healing.

> Attachment styles impact all kinds of relationships. In a marketing team, two employees, Alex and Jamie, had different attachment styles which often ended up causing problems. Alex, who had a secure attachment style, was comfortable working with others and liked to communicate openly. Jamie, on the other hand had an anxious attachment style, and often needed reassurance and worried about being left

out.

During a project, Jamie felt that Alex was not providing enough support. This made Jamie defensive, and he began to criticize Alex's work. This growing tension led to misunderstandings, missed deadlines, and a drop in team morale.

To resolve the issue, their manager set up a meeting where both could share their feelings and concerns. The manager helped Alex understand Jamie's need for reassurance and showed Jamie how to express his needs without becoming defensive.

By creating an environment of understanding and open talk, Alex learned to offer more support, while Jamie figured out how to communicate his needs more effectively. They decided to have regular check-ins to stay on track with the project and strengthen their working relationship. This solution not only improved their relationship but also positively affected the entire team.

Healthy Communication Techniques

Equipping yourself with the right tools for communication is key to building healthy relationships. When you express your feelings and needs clearly, you can avoid misunderstandings and strengthen your connections with others. Here are some practical strategies for enhancing communication in your relationships:

Active Listening

Active listening is essential for building stronger relationships and deeper understanding with your partner. It goes beyond merely hearing their words; it requires you to fully engage with what they are saying. To truly practice active listening, make sure to maintain eye contact, refrain from interrupting, and offer both verbal and non-verbal responses that show you're really paying attention.

Maintaining Eye Contact

Eye contact plays a crucial role in creating genuine connections during conversations. It conveys to your conversation partner that you are truly present and attentive to what they're sharing. You don't need to fixate intensely; instead, aim for a relaxed and steady gaze that reflects your interest and engagement.

Avoiding Interruptions

Interruptions can disrupt your partner's flow of ideas and might leave them feeling frustrated or disregarded. Practice holding your responses until your conversation partner has completed their thoughts. If you're concerned about forgetting your own points, consider jotting down quick notes to revisit later.

Providing Verbal and Non-Verbal Cues

Encouraging your partner by nodding, leaning in, or matching their gestures shows that you're genuinely listening. Simple phrases like "I understand" or "That makes sense" can further highlight your involvement and compassion.

Using 'I' Statements

I-statements are a powerful tool for sharing your feelings and needs without placing blame. This approach can help minimize defensiveness and encourage open conversations. Instead of saying, "You never listen to me," you could say, "I feel unheard when I speak, and I need us to improve our communication."

Articulation Without Blame

The goal is to focus on your own experience rather than placing blame on your partner. By framing your statements around your feelings and needs, you shift the conversation from a confrontational stance to a more constructive one. Instead of saying, "You never listen to me," you might express, "I feel unheard when I talk about my day." This approach not only fosters a deeper understanding between both partners but also encourages open communication. By sharing your feelings honestly, you create an environment where your partner feels safe to respond without feeling attacked. This openness can lead to greater empathy and a collaborative effort to resolve conflicts, ultimately strengthening the relationship.

Navigating Difficult Conversations

Difficult conversations are a part of every relationship, whether personal or work-related. These conversations often come from different views, unmet expectations, or misunderstandings, and they can easily lead to problems if not handled carefully. However, when we have these conversations with respect and understanding, we can reduce tension and create a space for open discussion. By listening to each other and acknowledging each other's feelings, we can turn tough moments into avenues of growth. This way, we not only strengthen our connections but also better understand each other's perspectives, leading to a stronger and more positive relationship. Seeing difficult conversations as important for connection helps us deal with misunderstandings easily, making room for personal and relational growth.

Strategies for Addressing Conflicts

Approaching difficult conversations calmly and respectfully helps create a positive atmosphere and leads to better discussions. When discussing sensitive subjects, plan out what you want to say beforehand. This helps you express your thoughts clearly and avoids speaking out of anger or frustration, which can hurt the conversation. Also, using "I" statements is important; it lets you share your feelings without sounding like you're blaming the other person. This keeps the discussion focused on finding a solution instead of arguing. By creating an environment of respect and understanding, you encourage open communication and the chance to find solutions together.

Preparing for Challenging Discussions

Preparation reduces anxiety. Think about the main points you want to address and possible solutions. Approach the conversation with an open mind and be willing to listen and adjust your perspective.

Practicing Gratitude in Communication

Regularly showing gratitude and compassion can profoundly strengthen the positivity and durability of our interpersonal connections. These practices foster an environment where individuals feel valued and understood, leading to deeper bonds and enhanced emotional resilience. By actively acknowledging one another's contributions and demonstrating kindness, we create a foundation of trust and support that can withstand challenges and grow over time.

Importance of Expressing Appreciation

Recognizing and appreciating the positive traits and actions of your partner creates a nurturing atmosphere. Expressing your appreciation, even for routine tasks like helping with chores, strengthens the bond of love and promotes mutual admiration. Small, heartfelt acknowledgments can significantly enhance the quality of your relationship, leaving both partners feeling valued and respected.

Cultivating Kindness

It is essential to develop the habit of acknowledging and celebrating your partner's efforts and contributions regularly. When you take the time to do this, it fosters an atmosphere where they feel cherished and recognized. This simple yet powerful practice does more than enhance your partner's self-worth; it also encourages a mutual exchange of appreciation that strengthens the bond you share. As this culture of positivity and support grows within your relationship, both partners will feel more motivated to contribute, creating a cycle of encouragement and love that can lead to a more fulfilling partnership.

Navigating Relationship Challenges from Past Wounds

Recognizing what makes you emotional is important for understanding how past experiences affect your relationships today. These emotional triggers often come from childhood—like neglect or trauma—and can show up in surprising ways now. For example, if someone raises their voice, it might remind you of a parent who yelled and how that made you feel, which could cause an overreaction in a discussion with your partner.

To find your triggers, think about what you feel during arguments or tense situations. Notice what makes you angry, scared, or sad. Keeping a journal can help you see patterns and figure out what specifically triggers these feelings. When you recognize these patterns, you might see that your reactions are tied to past events rather than what's happening now. This understanding is the first step towards responding better and building healthier relationships.

Once you know your triggers, managing them is key for steady relationships. One helpful technique is grounding, which keeps you focused on the present and helps reduce strong emotional reactions. Deep breathing can calm you down when you feel triggered. Another helpful method is progressive muscle relaxation, where you tense and then relax each muscle group to shift your focus from emotional pain to physical sensations, helping you gain control.

Establishing a routine for stressful moments can also help. Regular meditation can boost your ability to handle your emotions and stay mindful, making it easier to stay in the present instead of getting caught up in the past. Counting your breaths while inhaling deeply can be comforting too. Having these methods ready can help you respond quickly when you feel overwhelmed, stopping situations from getting worse.

Although looking back at past experiences can be scary, it's needed for healing. Unresolved issues can lead to ongoing problems and misunderstandings in your current relationships. Talking openly with your partner about past struggles can ease their impact on your life today. Start by identifying important unresolved issues you've faced. Write down these memories and their effects on you. Sharing this with your partner creates understanding, allowing both of you to deal with pain constructively.

Therapy is another helpful option. A therapist provides a safe space to explore past traumas while teaching you how to handle your feelings in a healthy way. Addressing these wounds with professional help can keep you from putting the responsibility of your healing on your partner, while you both work toward a healthier relationship.

Forgiveness is essential for freeing yourself from past hurts. Learning to forgive yourself and others can change your life, leading to freedom and better emotional health. Start by acknowledging any pain and anger you feel. Remember, forgiving doesn't mean excusing what happened; it's about releasing you from the emotional burden.

One useful way to encourage forgiveness is to write letters, whether to yourself or to those who have hurt you—sending them isn't even necessary. This allows you to express your feelings and lighten your emotional weight. Self-compassion is important too. Remind yourself that everyone makes mistakes and it's normal to feel hurt. Speaking kindly to yourself and using positive affirmations can help shift your mindset from resentment to acceptance and peace.

Including regular self-care in your routine helps your journey of forgiveness and emotional release. Activities like yoga, journaling, or enjoying hobbies provide moments of reflection and comfort. Connecting with supportive friends, family, or groups can also give you validation and new perspectives, making the process of forgiveness and emotional growth easier.

Building Trust and Intimacy in Relationships

To build healthy and meaningful relationships, you need to understand the tools that can boost trust and intimacy. These key elements come from being vulnerable, consistent in your actions, transparent with each other, being emotionally available, and sharing experiences.

The Importance of Vulnerability

Being vulnerable is vital for creating real connections. It means opening up about your fears, insecurities, and dreams without worrying about being judged or rejected. Vulnerability lets you and your partner see each other's true selves, which deepens intimacy. According to Marie (2022), being vulnerable is key to forming genuine connections because it invites others into your lives in a meaningful way. By sharing personal thoughts and feelings, you can create trust and understanding. This openness helps you both appreciate and support each other's emotions more deeply.

Consistent Actions and Transparency

Trust grows through consistent actions and clear communication. When you and your partner show reliable behavior and honest intentions, it creates a sense of safety. Trust isn't built in a day; it develops through dependable actions over time. Being consistent with your words and deeds helps both of you feel valued and supported. For example, checking in with each other regularly, keeping promises, and being truthful about your feelings helps establish trust. Transparency is also key; being open about your thoughts and intentions avoids misunderstandings and promotes honesty.

Emotional Availability

Being emotionally available means being present and responsive to your partner's needs. It involves actively listening and showing empathy during tough times. This means making an effort to understand and support how your partner feels. Whether you're celebrating their successes or comforting them when they're down, being emotionally available strengthens your bond. Techniques like maintaining eye contact, listening attentively, and expressing empathy through kind words can enhance this connection. It's important to be there for your partner when it matters most, providing comfort and understanding during difficult moments.

Creating Shared Experiences

Participating in shared activities is a fantastic way to build emotional connections and deepen intimacy. Whether it's simple daily tasks or exciting adventures, these experiences offer bonding opportunities. Activities like cooking together, traveling, or exploring hobbies create joyful memories. Engaging in enjoyable activities helps you work together, communicate well, and appreciate each other's company. By doing things you both love, you can create a wealth of positive experiences that form a strong and happy relationship.

Final Insights

Understanding how we connect with others is important for our relationships. By looking back at our childhood experiences, we can understand why we act the way we do with people. This understanding helps us be kinder to ourselves and to those we are close to. Knowing this gives us the tools to create better and safer relationships.

As we move ahead, we must remember that change requires time and effort. Learning new ways to connect and having healthier attachment styles takes patience and practice. Being open, acting consistently, and communicating well are essential for this change. By focusing on these things, we can build trust and deeper connections. Approach this journey with kindness, knowing that each step brings us closer to meaningful relationships.

As we work toward healthier connections, it's important to have effective ways to cope with challenges. Next, we will learn how to create these coping strategies and find practical tools to handle our emotions during tough times.

Developing Effective Coping Mechanisms

> "Peace is not something you wish for, it's something you make." - Robert Fulghum

Developing strong coping mechanisms requires you to recognize and address the emotional pain that can stem from past experiences. In this chapter, we'll explore a variety of practical approaches designed to help you effectively navigate your feelings and come out stronger. By pinpointing your unique triggers, you can equip yourself to face tough moments, turning potential difficulties into valuable opportunities for personal growth.

Recognizing and Managing Triggers

Understanding and managing emotional triggers is important, especially for trauma survivors. Emotional triggers are situations, words, or actions that provoke strong reactions connected to past experiences. By recognizing these triggers, you can better navigate your emotions and develop healthier coping strategies.

To identify your emotional triggers, reflect on when you felt strongly affected. Ask yourself questions like, “What caused my upset mood?” or “Did this remind me of something from the past?” These questions can help you understand your emotional responses. Keeping a mood diary is useful. By tracking your emotions and related events, you’ll identify patterns that reveal your triggers (Wright, 2023).

Once you've identified your triggers, create a Trigger Action Plan. This strategy will provide tools to manage triggering moments. Predict potential triggers and prepare responses. For example, if family gatherings cause anxiety, plan how to respond calmly. Techniques like deep breathing and positive self-talk can help ease anxiety. Practicing the Cope Ahead technique, where you mentally prepare for triggers, can also be beneficial (*10 Effective Strategies to Manage Overwhelming Emotions* , 2024).

Developing healthy responses to triggers turns emotional crises into growth opportunities. Knowing that an outburst can be managed restores your sense of control. Physical activities like exercise are great for releasing emotions. Creative outlets, such as painting or making music, provide constructive ways to express feelings. Mindfulness practices help manage reactions by keeping you present, reducing the intensity of emotional responses. Simple exercises, like focusing on your breath or doing a body scan, can help you respond more calmly (*Effective Strategies to Manage Overwhelming Emotions* , 2024).

Reflecting on your triggers is an ongoing process that supports healing. Keeping a reflective journal is helpful. Documenting your emotions related to triggers reveals recurring themes and patterns. For example, writing about feelings after an argument can expose issues tied to self-worth. Over time, journaling uncovers triggers and the origins of your emotional reactions, leading to healing.

Relaxation and Stress-Reduction Techniques

When dealing with emotional pain from past trauma, it's essential to find practical methods to relax. Effective relaxation techniques can greatly reduce stress and support your emotional healing process. In this section, you'll discover four key relaxation strategies: breathing exercises, progressive muscle relaxation, visualization exercises, and mindfulness practices.

Deep Breathing Exercises

Deep breathing is an effective and accessible technique for quickly easing stress. When you concentrate on your breath, you help to soothe your nervous system and foster a tranquil state of mind. To begin deep breathing, find a comfortable position—whether sitting or lying down. Gently close your eyes and inhale slowly through your nose, allowing your belly to rise fully. Hold your breath for a count of three, then exhale slowly through your mouth, releasing any tightness.

Repeat this process five to ten times, or until you feel calmer. Deep breathing not only helps manage immediate stress but also improves overall clarity and focus.

Progressive Muscle Relaxation

Progressive muscle relaxation (PMR) is a method that guides you through tensing and then relaxing various muscle groups in your body. This practice enhances your awareness of how tension and relaxation feel. To start, find a calm, private space where you can focus. Sit or lie down in a comfortable position and close your eyes. Begin with your toes, squeezing the muscles tightly for about five seconds, then gently let them go for 30 seconds, taking note of the difference between tension and relaxation. Gradually move up through your body—feet, calves, thighs, abdomen, chest, arms, hands, neck, and face. By the time you finish, you should notice a greater sense of relaxation throughout your entire body. Regular practice of PMR can significantly boost your ability to cope with stress and help you identify when tension arises.

Visualization Techniques

Visualization, often referred to as guided imagery, empowers you to harness your imagination to conjure a calming mental image that fosters relaxation and security. This technique leverages the incredible influence of your mind on your body's state. Start by choosing a cozy, tranquil spot to either sit or lie down comfortably. Close your eyes and picture a serene place that brings you peace—be it a tranquil beach, a lush forest, or any environment where you feel at ease and safe.

Immerse yourself in this visualization by engaging all your senses: hear the soothing sounds, breathe in the distinct aromas, observe the vibrant sights, and even feel the textures present in your imagined space. For instance, if you envision a beach, listen to the rhythmic waves, inhale the refreshing scent of the ocean, witness the sunlight glinting off the water, and savor the soft sand beneath your feet. Allow yourself several minutes to dwell in this vivid scene, fully absorbing the calm it provides. Visualization can be a powerful ally during stressful times, offering a swift refuge to soothe your mind and body.

Mindfulness Practices

Mindfulness means being fully present and aware of your thoughts, feelings, and physical sensations without passing judgment. Engaging in mindfulness exercises can significantly lessen the hold of past traumas on your current emotional state by promoting a deeper awareness and acceptance of your internal experiences. A straightforward way to cultivate mindfulness is through breath awareness. Find a comfortable position and gently close your eyes. Direct your attention to your breath as it flows in and out of your body. Notice the feeling of air entering your nose, filling your lungs, and exiting your body. If your mind drifts, just redirect your focus back to your breath.

Another helpful practice is the body scan, where you mentally examine your body from your head to your toes, identifying any areas of tension or discomfort, and intentionally easing those spots. Regularly practicing mindfulness can improve your emotional balance, lower stress, and enhance your overall well-being (Robinson, 2019).

Using Grounding Methods During Emotional Episodes

Grounding techniques are effective methods for managing strong emotions, especially after experiencing trauma. These practices anchor you in the present moment, serving as a barrier against troubling thoughts and feelings. We will now discuss easy ways to help you control your emotions and build strength in tough times.

The 5-4-3-2-1 Technique is a fundamental grounding exercise that helps shift your attention from internal turmoil to your external surroundings by utilizing your senses. Begin by identifying five visible items in your environment, focusing on specific details like wall patterns or sunlight streaming through a window. Next, identify four objects you can touch, paying attention to their texture and temperature—like the coolness of a metal surface or the softness of a blanket. Follow with three distinct sounds, such as birds chirping or the hum of a fan. Then, recognize two noticeable scents, whether it's the rich aroma of brewed coffee or fresh laundry. Finally, pinpoint one taste, such as chewing gum or a sip of water. Engaging with your environment through this sensory exercise can significantly reduce feelings of panic and disconnection, fostering tranquility and presence (Schuldt, 2022).

Safe Space Visualization involves creating a mental retreat for yourself during stressful times. Envision a comfortable place where you feel completely safe, whether it's a secluded beach, a cozy room, or a peaceful meadow. Bring this space to life in your mind by visualizing its colors, shapes, and layout. Fill in additional details, like the sound of crashing waves, the scent of pine trees, or the warmth of sunlight on your skin. Regularly practicing this visualization establishes a mental refuge that you can access at any time to help you regain composure and emotional control (Raypole, 2019).

Physical Grounding Techniques focus on bodily sensations and movements to keep you present. One simple method is to hold an object, like a stone or a sturdy piece of furniture. Concentrate on its texture, weight, and warmth in your grip. Walking can also be an effective grounding practice. Pay attention to each step, feeling your feet touch the ground and the rhythm of your movement. Actions like stretching, pressing your feet into the floor while seated, or feeling the chair's support against your back can act as physical anchors. These methods help divert your attention away from distressing thoughts, promoting a sense of stability and grounding.

Breath Focus in Grounding combines breathing exercises with mindfulness to bring clarity during challenging emotions. Start by taking slow, deep breaths. Inhale deeply through your nose, letting your abdomen expand, and then gently exhale through your mouth. Focus on the sensations of your breath: the rise and fall of your chest, the cool air entering your nostrils, and the warmth as you exhale. You can enhance this practice by counting each breath, which helps maintain concentration. Practicing breath focus not only calms your nervous system but also boosts the effectiveness of other grounding techniques, making it easier to stay present and manage overwhelming feelings.

Incorporating these grounding techniques into your daily routine creates a personal toolkit for emotional strength. Regular practice makes these strategies more accessible and effective when needed. For instance, using the 5-4-3-2-1 Technique during moments of anxiety can quickly shift your focus to comforting sensory experiences. Similarly, having a well-established Safe Space Visualization can provide immediate solace in stressful situations. Physical techniques like holding a familiar object or focusing on your steps can blend seamlessly into your daily activities, offering consistent opportunities to regain balance. Breath Focus is discreet and can be practiced anywhere, delivering quick relief when emotions become overwhelming.

Mastering these grounding techniques requires patience and practice. Different methods may resonate with you at different times, so feel free to explore and discover what works best for you. Tailor your grounding practices to fit your preferences and situations. The aim is to find reliable strategies that foster a sense of safety, control, and presence, even during life's emotional challenges.

Practicing grounding techniques regularly, even when feeling calm, strengthens their effectiveness. This proactive approach ensures that when intense emotions arise, you have well-practiced skills ready to assist you. Furthermore, combining various techniques can create a comprehensive grounding experience. For example, blending breath focus with Safe Space Visualization can enhance the calming effects, producing a powerful synergy that stabilizes your emotional state.

> Jenny, a 45-year-old graphic designer, found herself overwhelmed by intense emotional reactions at work and at home. Her

childhood, marked by emotional neglect, left her with deep feelings of inadequacy and unworthiness. Minor setbacks or criticisms would trigger strong, intense responses.

At work, constructive feedback and tight deadlines would send Jenny into a spiral of stress, affecting her productivity. At home, even small disagreements with family would quickly escalate, straining her relationships.

In therapy, Jenny discovered the power of visualization. She created a mental sanctuary —a calming place she could visit whenever her emotions flared up. This simple practice allowed her to step back, breathe deeply, and regain her composure.

Whenever she faced a stressful moment, Jenny would close her eyes and transport herself to this peaceful mental space. Over time, this technique not only helped her handle immediate stress but also softened the impact of her emotional triggers.

Jenny's use of visualization brought significant change. She became more balanced and calm, enhancing her

> performance at work and fostering better relationships at home. Her journey shows how a simple mental tool can make a profound difference, helping anyone navigate life's stresses with greater ease and emotional resilience.

Incorporating Self-Care Routines into Daily Life

Creating a self-care routine is crucial for your physical and emotional health. If you've faced trauma in the past, a consistent routine can bring a sense of stability and control. In this section, you'll discover various elements of self-care and how they can help you cope effectively.

Begin by identifying activities that make you feel good and promote relaxation. Regular exercise, healthy eating, and adequate sleep are the cornerstones of well-being. Engaging in physical activities like walking, practicing yoga, or dancing not only lifts your spirits but also energizes you to tackle daily challenges. By consistently scheduling these activities, you create a comforting and predictable environment, especially beneficial for those who have experienced trauma. A consistent routine reduces uncertainty, making it easier to handle stress and anxiety (Manzo, 2024).

Building this routine is more than crossing items off a checklist; it involves thoughtful intention and self-reflection. Set small, attainable goals so you don't feel overwhelmed. For example, start with a simple morning routine that includes drinking warm water, stretching, and journaling. As you grow more comfortable, gradually incorporate additional activities. Regularly reviewing and adjusting your routine helps it stay aligned with your evolving needs.

Your self-care activities should be as unique as you are. There's no universal approach to self-care—what uplifts one person may not resonate with another. That's why it's essential to explore various activities until you find what feels right for you. Some people find joy in creative pursuits like painting or writing, while others may prefer time spent outdoors or practicing mindfulness. Pursuing hobbies that bring you happiness can significantly alleviate daily stress.

This variety of activities helps you adjust to how you feel, giving you different ways to relax and manage stress. Being flexible with your self-care is important. Your emotional needs can change, so your self-care methods should change too. When you're anxious or feeling overwhelmed, calming activities like deep breathing or listening to soft music can help you feel more centered. On days when you have low energy, try more active things like a brisk walk or dancing to boost your mood. By paying attention to your emotions, you are building strength and improving your ability to cope. This flexibility ensures that self-care remains effective in diverse circumstances (Northwestern Medicine, 2016).

Making self-care a priority is important for your mental health. Many people forget to take care of themselves because they are busy or focused on taking care of others. However, putting yourself first is not selfish; it's an important investment in your happiness and health. Set aside time for self-care activities just like you would for important appointments. Treat these moments for yourself with the same importance as meetings or doctor's visits to show that you care about your well-being.

Adding mindfulness to your self-care can make it even more effective. Activities like meditation and guided relaxation help you become more aware of yourself and reduce stress. These practices encourage you to pay attention to the present and to notice your thoughts and feelings without judging them. Mindfulness can help create balance in your emotions and bring a calm mindset. Start with simple techniques, such as focusing on your breath or noticing your senses during daily tasks, to easily include mindfulness in your routine.

A key part of good self-care is setting boundaries. Learn to say no and protect your time and energy to stay balanced. Setting limits can help you avoid burnout and make sure you have enough energy to take care of yourself. This might mean skipping social events when you need rest or sharing tasks when you feel overwhelmed. Clearly stating your boundaries shows others what you need and helps build healthier relationships.

Celebrate your successes along the way to strengthen your commitment to self-care. Recognize the effort you put into your routine, whether you've completed a week of regular exercise, managed stress well, or taken time for yourself. Acknowledging these achievements boosts your confidence and motivation. Celebrations don't have to be big; even small rewards, like enjoying a favorite snack or taking a relaxing bath, can remind you of your commitment to self-care.

Summary and Reflections

This chapter empowered you to identify and manage emotional triggers. By understanding these triggers and devising a Trigger Action Plan, you can navigate challenges with greater ease. Techniques like mood journaling and mindfulness keep you grounded and present, fostering healthier emotional responses and enhancing self-awareness. Integrating relaxation methods into your daily routine—such as deep breathing and visualization—supports emotional regulation and resilience. Consistent practice of these strategies builds a strong emotional foundation, enabling you to face life's challenges with confidence.

As we embark on the next phase of our journey towards healing your inner child, you'll discover the transformative power of connecting with supportive communities that can elevate your emotional well-being and inspire your healing process.

Creating a Supportive Community

> "Alone, we can do so little; together, we can do so much." – Helen Keller

Creating a supportive community is essential for healing from childhood trauma. These nurturing connections can bring you comfort, affirm your feelings, and motivate you as you deal with the challenging emotions tied to recovery. When you are with people who genuinely understand your struggles, it becomes simpler to face and heal from your past wounds.

Finding and Joining Support Groups

Navigating the path to healing from childhood trauma can feel overwhelming, but connecting with a supportive community can make a significant difference. One effective way to do this is by joining a support group. In this section, you'll learn how to find and engage in groups that offer the emotional support and understanding essential for your healing journey.

Support groups come in various types. You can find local meetings, online forums, or sessions led by mental health experts. Each type has its own benefits. In-person groups allow for direct interaction, helping you make real connections. Online groups are flexible and can be accessed from anywhere, which is helpful if you live far away or have a busy schedule. Groups led by professionals offer structured support that focuses on specific issues or goals.

Finding the right support group might take some time. Start by checking local community centers, churches, or libraries, as these places often host or advertise in-person groups. Social media, especially Facebook, can also be a treasure trove for finding both local and online communities. Many local groups focus on specific issues like anxiety, depression, or trauma recovery. Mental health websites connected to reputable organizations typically maintain directories of support groups available to you.

Meetup is a great way to find groups that fit your needs. If you want support or to talk about a specific experience, Meetup helps you connect with people who understand what you're going through.

Facebook also has private groups where members can share their stories in a safe place. These sites not only help you find groups but also let you see how the community interacts and stays active.

When considering a support group, it's important to see if it aligns with your healing goals and comfort levels. Attend a few sessions to understand the group dynamics. Are the discussions relevant to your situation? Do you feel safe and accepted? Trust your feelings; if something seems off, it might not be the right match for you, and that's completely fine. It's okay to explore different groups until you find one that truly supports you.

Knowing the types of support groups available can help you make an informed decision. Peer-led groups often create a sense of camaraderie and shared understanding, as everyone shares their own stories and insights. This environment encourages deep connections and empathy. In contrast, professional-led groups focus on expert guidance and structured methods for addressing trauma, which can be particularly helpful if you're seeking advice based on psychological principles.

One vital factor to consider while exploring options is the size and frequency of meetings. Smaller groups often create a more personal atmosphere conducive to forming close relationships, while larger ones can provide a wider array of perspectives. Meeting frequency is also crucial; some groups gather weekly, while others meet less often. Think about what regularity will best support your healing process and suit your lifestyle.

Local mental health organizations, such as those associated with Mental Health America, can help you find groups in your area. They maintain directories and can give recommendations tailored to your needs. Additionally, national hotlines and online databases can guide you toward specialized groups covering topics like substance abuse, grief recovery, or chronic illness management.

In recent years, online support groups have gained popularity and offer a valuable option. Websites like Support Groups Central curate various groups from reputable organizations, allowing you to search for topics that resonate with you. The Dinner Party, for example, connects young adults processing loss, enabling them to gather in small, nurturing groups. Such resources expand your choices beyond geographical limits.

Support groups can help you heal, but they may not replace professional therapy. The effectiveness of these groups can be different for everyone. Always put your well-being first, and if a group doesn't help you, look for other options. Professional mental health care should be a key part of your healing process, along with the support you get from others.

Walking into a support group for the first time can be scary. But sharing experiences and learning from others in these groups can bring a lot of comfort. Realizing that others have faced similar problems can give you hope and show you that you're not alone. Take your time to find the right group that fits your healing journey.

Building a Personal Support Network

Cultivating a network of supportive friends, family, and professionals is vital for healing your inner child. This network offers emotional backing, practical advice, and encouragement that are essential as you navigate your journey toward recovery.

Start by recognizing who truly cares about your well-being. Close friends and family often play significant roles in offering invaluable emotional support. They understand you well, know your personal history, and can provide empathy and encouragement. Supportive friends understand your emotional triggers and can guide you through challenging moments. Family members offer a crucial sense of security and belonging that supports your healing journey.

Building strong relationships relies on genuine communication. Share your thoughts openly, and be an attentive listener. When discussing your feelings, articulate your experiences and specify how others can support you. This openness cultivates trust and deepens connections. Additionally, expressing gratitude, such as a sincere "thank you," can greatly enhance your relationships.

Establishing healthy boundaries is vital for sustaining personal relationships. Boundaries define acceptable interactions and safeguard your emotional health. They allow you to manage external pressures effectively, promoting a balanced exchange of support. For instance, if a friend frequently unloads their issues onto you without reciprocating, it's essential to set limits. Clearly articulating these boundaries helps others recognize your needs and fosters mutual respect.

Strong, supportive relationships play a crucial role in managing stress. Research highlights numerous benefits of a solid social support system, including enhanced health, longevity, and overall well-being (University at Buffalo, 2024).

To nurture these important relationships, practice give and take. Be available for your friends as they are for you. Show appreciation regularly, maintain contact through conversations, and return invitations. Be present in tough times, listen without judgment, and accept help when offered. While relying on others may feel uncomfortable, allowing friends and family to support you creates balance and signifies your appreciation for their involvement.

Celebrate your friends' achievements and maintain open communication to strengthen these bonds. Acknowledge their successes genuinely and promptly resolve any misunderstandings. Assume that any mistakes are unintentional and seek clarification to maintain harmony. Graciously accept apologies and respect each other's boundaries regarding social interactions.

Recognizing when a relationship is detrimental to your well-being is essential for preserving a supportive network. Relationships that drain your energy or involve criticism can impede your healing process. Such dynamics tend to increase stress rather than alleviate it. As a key aspect of self-care, remember that not everyone needs to be part of your life, especially those who are toxic. Releasing such individuals safeguards your well-being and ensures your support system uplifts you (Building a Support Network: The Art of Cultivating Friends Who Have Your Back, n.d.).

Lastly, think about the friendships you've built. What makes some of them important to you? Are these friends reliable? Do they help you feel good? It's better to have a few strong connections than many weak ones. Spend your time on relationships that help you grow and heal.

Sharing and Connecting with Others

Creating a caring community is important for healing, especially when it comes to your inner child. Sharing your stories helps to connect with others and brings hope. Whether you talk about your successes or struggles, your experiences help fight loneliness and build a sense of belonging. When you share what you've been through, you show others that their feelings are valid and encourage them on their healing journey.

Having deep conversations is a great way to strengthen these connections. Starting these talks can be scary, but there are simple ways to make it easier. Create a welcoming space where everyone feels safe to share without being judged. Small groups, either in person or online, help people connect more deeply. At these gatherings, share your own stories first to make it easier for others to open up.

When organizing these small meetings, think about who might benefit from them. It can help to have a specific topic for each session, so there's a clear focus. Finding a balance between having a plan and allowing natural conversation lets everyone participate meaningfully. Encourage sharing by asking open-ended questions like, "What has been a key challenge in your healing journey?"

Social media can also be a great way to find support and community. Online groups focused on healing and personal growth provide a chance to connect with others who have similar experiences. This creates a sense of community even if you can't meet in person. By engaging in these groups, you can share your story and support others as well. Join in by commenting, encouraging others, and sharing helpful resources. These interactions build a support network that goes beyond physical distance.

To get the most out of social media, try joining different groups to find the ones that feel right for you. Not every group will be a perfect fit, and that's okay. Look for groups that promote a positive and respectful environment where members support each other. When the group has good energy, it helps everyone stay motivated. Also, use event features on platforms to organize virtual meetups for real-time connections.

Having a mentor is another important part of a supportive community. Finding mentors who can support your healing can offer guidance, motivation, and inspiration. Look for people who have gone through similar challenges and can share their experiences. You can find mentors in support groups, professional circles, or personal relationships. Building a relationship with a mentor involves being open about your goals and challenges, which helps them provide personalized advice.

To find a mentor effectively, start by identifying what you need in your healing journey. Are you looking for specific therapeutic methods or emotional support? Once you know what you're seeking, reach out to potential mentors with a clear request. Be honest about why you think they would be a good mentor and express your desire to learn and grow. Remember, the mentor-mentee relationship should help both of you grow and feel better.

By sharing your stories and building connections, you can turn your healing journey into a shared experience. You'll realize that you're not alone in your struggles, and that support and hope are within reach. Whether through meaningful conversations, group meetings, social media interactions, or mentorship, creating a supportive community can significantly enhance your emotional healing and personal development. Nurturing these connections leads to a shared journey filled with understanding, empathy, and resilience.

Fostering a Sense of Community and Belonging

Belonging is a core human need and plays a significant role in your recovery from past traumas. When you feel a genuine sense of belonging, you naturally build the emotional strength needed for healing. This feeling is particularly vital as you work to heal the inner child still affected by childhood wounds.

Belonging acts as a shield during stressful times. It offers the emotional support that nurtures resilience and strengthens your capacity to face challenges. The encouragement you receive from your community confirms your worth and adds depth to your healing journey. Feeling understood and accepted by others reduces the isolation and loneliness often linked to trauma, making your recovery seem more manageable.

Creating inclusive environments enhances your sense of belonging. Communities that welcome diversity support collective healing, ensuring everyone feels their experiences are valued. Empathy should drive every interaction in these spaces. This means genuinely listening to others' stories without judgment, allowing everyone to express their feelings freely.

Participating in local activities, like workshops and volunteering, is key to building community support. Mental health and trauma recovery workshops provide practical healing tools and opportunities to connect with like-minded individuals. These gatherings serve as educational resources and spaces where meaningful bonds can develop.

Volunteering in your community is another powerful way to establish a support network.

Engaging in local projects allows you to contribute positively while fostering friendships and encouragement through collective efforts. This involvement creates a sense of purpose and belonging, key elements in strengthening your emotional resilience. Taking part in community initiatives or local events can help you forge closer connections and feel part of something larger (Sandberg et al, 2024).

Once you join a community, it's essential to remain engaged in its activities. Engagement goes beyond mere participation; it involves becoming an active member. Regularly connecting with your support system strengthens relationships and showcases your dedication to healing. Attending meetings, participating in activities, and keeping communication open ensures that your connections are solid and beneficial.

Getting involved requires time and effort. Feeling nervous initially is normal, especially when sharing personal stories. Knowing what to anticipate can ease your anxiety about engaging with new groups. Setting realistic expectations for your early interactions is crucial, as building trust and comfort takes time. These activities are ongoing; they play a crucial role in providing emotional support.

Communities thrive on shared support and experiences. Being part of a community allows you to gain insights from others' strengths, which can inspire you. Healing together occurs when individuals partake in activities that foster connection and growth. Be it organized events, casual meet-ups, or collaborative projects, these experiences cultivate a supportive atmosphere.

Online platforms can also help you build and maintain your support network. Websites, social media, and virtual workshops connect you with others who may lack local resources. These online environments enhance your support system, providing ample opportunities for connections and understanding. They enable participation from the comfort of your home, which can be beneficial if in-person interactions feel challenging.

Effective communication is vital for nurturing these support networks. Honest discussions build trust and fortify relationships. Active listening and expressing gratitude for received support create a positive and reciprocal environment. Good communication also addresses misunderstandings, ensuring the community remains safe and supportive for everyone involved.

Recognizing and celebrating progress is crucial, both individually and collectively. Acknowledging achievements motivates positive actions and intensifies the community's commitment to healing together. Celebrations can range from simple acknowledgments during meetings to hosting special events that showcase the group's milestones. These moments uplift morale and help sustain high engagement levels.

Final Thoughts

As you move forward, remember the vital role supportive networks play in healing your wounded inner child. Exploring various options might take some time, but finding the right fit can provide invaluable emotional backing for your journey. Focus on how you feel in these groups—whether they match your personal goals and comfort levels. This will help you find the community that best supports your healing.Remember, the goal is not just about finding any support, but the right support that encourages and uplifts you through every step of your healing journey.

As we embark on our journey towards emotional wellness, it is vital to integrate transformative healing practices into our daily routines, paving the way for enduring growth and resilience. The next chapter will integrate and enhance the knowledge we've acquired, ensuring it becomes an inherent aspect of our daily lives.

Sustaining Long-term Growth and Resilience

> "Life doesn't get easier or more forgiving, we get stronger and more resilient." - Steve Maraboli

Sustaining long-term growth and resilience involves incorporating healing practices into your daily life. By weaving these practices into your routine, you can effectively address emotional wounds, strengthen your emotional resilience, and maintain a balanced mental state. The goal is to cultivate habits that promote emotional well-being and resilience, making your journey of healing both practical and attainable.

Integrating Healing Practices into Daily Life

We will now look at some effective techniques and how you can seamlessly integrate them into your life for ongoing personal development.

Mindfulness Practices

Practicing mindfulness every day can improve your emotional awareness and presence. Mindfulness is about being fully present without judgment. For those with childhood trauma and abuse, staying in the present can be tough but rewarding. You can start with simple actions like mindful breathing or spending a few minutes observing your thoughts without reacting; these can lead to significant changes. Mindfulness journaling is another effective way to reflect on your feelings and thoughts, leading to better understanding and processing (Greenslade, 2024). Over time, these habits can improve emotional regulation, reduce stress, and create a greater sense of calm.

Creating specific rituals can help you make mindfulness a regular part of your life. Set up a quiet space at home for consistent practice. Start and end your day with a short mindfulness session, even if it's just five minutes of deep breathing or a guided meditation. These moments of presence help you during the chaos of daily life and build a foundation of peace and clarity. You can also incorporate mindfulness into daily activities—like eating, walking, or washing dishes—turning these tasks into meaningful practices. The key is to fully engage with each activity, paying attention to the sights, sounds, smells, and textures around you.

Self-reflection Techniques

Regularly thinking about your feelings helps you understand them better. When you take time to reflect, you can notice patterns in your behavior, see what makes you feel a certain way, and find things in your life that you want to improve. One good way to do this is by keeping a journal where you write down your daily experiences, emotions, and thoughts. You can use prompts like "What challenge did I face today?", "What emotions did I feel?", and "What can I learn from this?" to help guide your thoughts. This practice not only helps you gain insight but also lets you see how you've grown over time, making you feel accomplished.

Spending time alone in nature or a quiet place also supports your self-reflection. Whether you take a walk in a garden or relax in a calm spot with a nice view, being alone helps you avoid distractions and connect with yourself. During these times, accept all your emotions without judging them; this helps you be kinder to yourself. Over time, regular self-reflection will help you understand yourself better, leading to better decision-making and emotional balance.

Routine Self-care Activities

Incorporating self-care into your daily life greatly improves your physical and emotional health. Self-care is not just about occasional treats; it's about developing regular habits that support your well-being. Regular exercise, enough sleep, healthy meals, and staying hydrated are key parts of self-care. By sticking to these habits, you help your body function better, which positively affects your mental and emotional health.

Besides these basics, make time for things that bring you joy and help you relax. Engage in hobbies like gardening, reading, or painting to boost your creativity. Physical activities like yoga or dancing also help with self-care, providing physical benefits and mental relief. Creating a calming bedtime routine, such as reading a good book, taking a warm bath, or listening to soft music, can greatly improve your sleep quality, which is essential for your overall health.

Self-care also involves understanding your limits and knowing when to say no. By protecting your energy and time from too many requests, you can focus on what really matters to you, helping you avoid burnout. When you make self-care a priority, you're signaling to yourself and others that your health is important, which strengthens your self-esteem and resilience.

Positive Affirmations

Regularly practicing affirmations can turn negative self-talk into positive thoughts. Affirmations are empowering statements you repeat to counteract self-defeating thoughts. For instance, phrases like "I deserve love and respect," "I can handle any challenges," and "I am worthy of happiness" can help rewire your brain for a better self-view (Staff, 2024).

To include affirmations in your daily routine, set aside specific times for them, such as during morning rituals or before bed. Writing affirmations on sticky notes and placing them where you can see them can serve as reminders throughout the day. Adding them to mindfulness exercises or journaling can increase their effectiveness.

When creating affirmations, choose phrases that match your goals and aspirations. Making them personal enhances their significance. Although it might feel strange at first, persistence is key; over time, these affirmations can impact your subconscious positively.

Incorporating these practices into your life supports personal growth. While it may be tough to find time or maintain consistency, starting with small steps can lead to significant changes. Explore different techniques to find what suits you best. Remember, the journey towards healing and growth is ongoing, and regularly practicing these methods is essential for resilience and well-being.

Setting Long-term Personal Growth Goals

For many, setting and pursuing long-term personal growth goals can seem daunting, but the rewards are immense. Linking these goals with your healing journey provides clarity and speeds up emotional recovery. Adopting a structured approach—utilizing models like SMART goals, crafting vision boards, engaging accountability partners, and remaining flexible—creates a foundation for sustained growth and resilience.

SMART Goals Framework

The SMART framework is an effective method for defining clear, achievable long-term goals. SMART represents specific, measurable, attainable, relevant, and time-bound. These guidelines make sure that each goal is clear and achievable within a set time, providing a direct path to what you want to achieve.

Specific : Goals need to be clear and direct. Rather than saying, "I want to improve my mental health," express it as, "I will dedicate 10 minutes each day to mindfulness meditation to reduce my stress."

Measurable: Introducing measurable components allows you to track your progress more effectively. Setting milestones, like "I will meditate every day for the next three months," provides a tangible measure of success.

Attainable : While it's crucial to challenge yourself, your goals must remain practical to avoid feelings of defeat. If you're new to meditation, beginning with a small daily commitment and gradually increasing it may be a more effective strategy.

Relevant : Your objectives should resonate with your overarching life dreams and values. Focusing on goals that support your emotional recovery and well-being ensures they have genuine meaning for you.

Time-bound : Setting deadlines creates urgency and clarity. By specifying your timeline, such as "I will integrate daily mindfulness meditation into my routine for three months," you maintain momentum and can monitor your progress. (What Is a Long-Term Goal and How Can I Achieve It? n.d.)

Vision Board Creation

Visualization is a potent technique in goal-setting that helps manifest your aspirations. Crafting a vision board filled with images, words, and symbols that embody your dreams serves as a constant reminder of what you aim to achieve. This visual representation fuels motivation and aligns you with your long-term goals.

To create a vision board, gather materials—magazines, photographs, quotes, or craft supplies. Select images and phrases that reflect your personal growth and healing journey. Organize these items on a physical or digital board, placing it where you can see it often. By regularly reviewing this collection of aspirations, you keep your intentions vivid and reignite your motivation each day.

Accountability Partners

Partnering with an accountability ally greatly enhances your capacity to set and accomplish long-term goals. This individual—whether a trusted peer, family member, therapist, or coach—understands your objectives and supports your progress. Regular check-ins foster commitment and motivation while providing opportunities for reflection, feedback, and encouragement.

By sharing your goals with someone else, you add a layer of external accountability that drives consistent action. Discussing your progress and challenges keeps your goals at the forefront of your mind. Additionally, an accountability partner can offer fresh insights, helping you navigate obstacles more effectively and allowing for greater celebration of your achievements.

Adapting to Change

Life is often unpredictable, and your path to personal growth is no exception. Adapting your goals is crucial for continued progress and resilience amid change. Flexibility allows you to reassess and modify your objectives when situations evolve, rather than succumbing to discouragement following setbacks.

Regularly reviewing and refining your goals is an effective method for preparing for change. This practice involves monitoring your progress, identifying obstacles, and contemplating alternative strategies. Cultivating coping mechanisms beforehand strengthens your resolve when unexpected challenges arise. Embracing flexibility doesn't mean relinquishing your aspirations; it involves seeking new ways to pursue them as life shifts. (How to Set Professional Goals for Yourself (with 11 Examples), n.d.)

Maintaining Motivation and Commitment

Exploring effective ways to maintain motivation and dedication to your personal growth is crucial during your healing process. Discovering what drives you can transform your life, particularly when coping with past trauma or unresolved emotional issues related to relationships.

Regular check-ins with yourself are important for staying motivated. Taking time to look at your progress helps you stay involved in the process. These reviews help you celebrate your wins, spot areas to improve, and change your goals if needed. Setting aside specific times each week or month for these reflections keeps your growth active and engaging, helping you stay focused on your long-term goals.

Developing a reward system can also increase your motivation significantly. Life's pressures can often feel overwhelming, and the journey of personal growth might seem challenging. By creating a system that celebrates small milestones, you foster positive reinforcement.

Rewards don't need to be extravagant; they can be as simple as savoring a favorite treat, enjoying a relaxing bath, or wholeheartedly diving into a cherished hobby. It's essential to recognize your achievements and appreciate the effort invested in your growth. This strategy not only boosts your motivation but also makes the journey enjoyable and less daunting.

Engaging with new materials fuels your growth mindset. Personal development is not a one-time effort; it's an ongoing journey. By actively seeking out new books, attending workshops, or joining webinars, you embrace a variety of ideas and viewpoints. This consistent exposure cultivates a lasting passion for growth, equipping you with diverse strategies for your journey. For instance, exploring different healing techniques or listening to those who have overcome similar challenges can provide valuable insights and renewed enthusiasm. Lifelong learning enables you to tackle new obstacles while reinforcing your dedication to self-improvement.

Embracing a growth mindset, as highlighted by Carol Dweck (Dweck, 2016), builds resilience during tough times. This mindset acknowledges that skills and intelligence can evolve through effort and commitment. This attitude fosters a genuine passion for learning and the perseverence needed to achieve meaningful goals. By adopting this viewpoint, you start to see setbacks as chances to grow rather than indicators of failure. This shift helps you focus on what you can achieve through hard work and determination. Regularly practicing this mindset allows you to navigate challenges more effectively.

Incorporating these strategies into your life creates a solid foundation for lasting motivation and commitment. Periodic self-assessments keep you engaged with your goals, encouraging accountability and informed adjustments. Rewarding yourself adds positivity to the process, ensuring that every step forward feels significant and worthy of recognition. Continuous learning injects excitement into personal development, recharging your motivation with new insights and enthusiasm. Ultimately, adopting a growth mindset empowers you to face challenges head-on, turning potential setbacks into opportunities for advancement.

For those healing from childhood trauma or dealing with unresolved emotional challenges, these techniques can be especially helpful. They address issues like feelings of being stuck, loss of motivation, and the overwhelming nature of long-term emotional healing. By implementing these strategies, you create a sustainable pathway to personal growth that respects your unique experiences while opening the door to profound transformation.

Routine self-assessments provide a stabilizing influence throughout the healing process. They promote regular reflection, ensuring that past efforts are recognized and future goals are clear. This practice can be grounding, offering a sense of control and direction.

Reward systems bring joy and celebration into the demanding journey of personal growth. They break the path into smaller, achievable milestones, each paired with a reward. This method alleviates the psychological weight of long-term ambitions, transforming them into reachable accomplishments.

Lifelong learning keeps your curiosity and drive alive. Engaging with new content ensures your intellectual and emotional investment in your journey. Whether through reading new literature, participating in workshops, or taking online courses, each piece of information deepens your understanding and enhances your skills.

Celebrating Progress and Milestones in the Healing Journey

Recognizing and celebrating your achievements during healing is important for lasting growth and strength. Even small victories can make you feel accomplished and motivated. Lets explore some simple ways to include this practice in your life.

Creating a visual map of your progress, known as Milestone Mapping, is a helpful tool. By marking key events or achievements on a timeline, you can clearly see your journey. This visual reminder helps keep you motivated and focused on your goals. Imagine placing important moments—like finishing a therapy program, improving relationships, or celebrating sobriety milestones—on a map. Each mark shows your strength and commitment, providing support during hard times.

Participating in Reflective Celebrations is another important way to acknowledge your progress. These celebrations don't need to be elaborate; they just need to be meaningful. Simple activities, like writing a letter to yourself about your efforts, enjoying a fun activity, or spending time with friends and family, can strengthen your sense of achievement. These moments help you appreciate the significance of your milestones.

Keeping a Personal Journal is very helpful for recognizing and reflecting on your achievements. Having a journal to record your successes allows you to note the details of each milestone, encouraging self-reflection and gratitude. Writing about your experiences helps process emotions, spot patterns, and understand the meaning of each step forward. For example, journaling about the challenges you overcame shows your resilience and determination. Over time, these reflections create a powerful story of your healing journey, inspiring you to continue on your path.

Sharing your milestones with a supportive community can greatly boost your accountability and motivation. When you talk about your achievements with trusted friends, family, or support groups, you enable collective celebration. This shared experience builds a sense of community and encouragement, reminding you that you're not alone in your journey. The praise and support from others can increase your confidence and inspire you to keep moving forward.

Final Insights

In this chapter, we looked at how important it is to include healing practices in our daily lives to help us grow and stay strong over time. We discussed simple techniques like being mindful, reflecting on ourselves, taking care of ourselves, and using positive affirmations. These methods can help us deal with stress, understand our feelings better, and create a balanced state of mind. By regularly using these practices, even if just a little at a time, you will see meaningful improvements in your overall well-being and emotional strength.

As we continue our journey of healing and personal growth, it's important to remember that this process is different for everyone and takes time. Being patient and kind to ourselves while using these practices can really help us as we move forward. Give yourself room to try different things and find what works best for you, knowing that every small step toward healing helps build a stronger and more satisfying life.

Conclusion

As we reach the end of this journey, let's take a moment to think about the main ideas we've discovered. Throughout this book, we've looked at how important it is to heal our inner child—part of us that holds onto past hurts and feelings we haven't dealt with. By recognizing and understanding this part, we've started a process of deep healing, personal growth, and emotional strength.

Remember when we first talked about the inner child? It was eye-opening to realize that this inner self is connected to many of your current emotional struggles. By recognizing and accepting your inner child, you started a big change. Healing your inner child isn't just about fixing old wounds; it's also about finding joy and being true to yourself. This awareness helps you live more genuinely, letting go of the pain and defenses built up over time.

Healing is an ongoing journey that requires patience, self-kindness, and determination. There will be good days and tough days. Some days, you might feel like you are making great progress, while other times, it may seem like nothing is happening. But remember: every small step you take is a victory on your journey to wholeness. Treat yourself with kindness and understand that the journey is just as important as the destination.

Personal growth is not a straight path. It's filled with unexpected twists, clear moments, and times of confusion. Throughout this book, you've been encouraged to explore different parts of your emotional health, to challenge old habits, and to welcome new ways of thinking and feeling. Each effort contributes to your healing and helps build a stronger foundation for future growth.

While individual effort is important, the support of a community matters just as much. One key idea we've discussed is the value of seeking support and connecting with others. You don't have to navigate this journey alone. Being around others on similar paths can provide encouragement, understanding, and shared wisdom. Imagine finding a support group where you feel truly understood, creating a safe space to heal and grow together. Sharing your experiences and listening to others can make the journey feel less overwhelming and more enriching.

Throughout this book, you have found practical tools to help your growth. You learnt simple yet effective techniques to improve your relationships and navigate relationship challenges. Techniques like journaling, setting boundaries, practicing mindfulness, and self-compassion exercises are valuable resources. These aren't just quick fixes; they are ongoing practices that you can add to your daily routine. For example, journaling each day lets you communicate with your inner child, giving it the care it has missed. Setting healthy boundaries helps you protect your emotional well-being and creates spaces that support your healing.

As you move forward, remember that the techniques you've learned are yours to keep and grow. They are the seeds of change planted throughout your reading—nurture them, and watch as they lead to healthier relationships and a stronger sense of self. Take a moment to reflect on how, by practicing self-compassion, you've already begun to change your relationship with your inner child from neglect to care.

These practices can help ground you during tough times. Whether it's taking a few minutes to breathe deeply, writing your thoughts down, or reaching out to a supportive friend, these actions show your commitment to your emotional health and strength. Over time, they become natural, showing your dedication to yourself and your journey.

Remember, you are not alone in this. Many others are on similar paths, facing their fears and working towards emotional well-being. By sharing your story, you also add to a larger narrative of healing and hope. Together, we can overcome past trauma and build a community of strength and resilience.

As you finish this book, take with you the lessons learned and insights gained. Let them comfort and motivate you. Think about how far you've come and look forward to the growth that lies ahead. The healing journey is ongoing, but each day offers new chances for joy, learning, and deeper connections with yourself and others.

In conclusion, recognize the strength it took to start this journey. Celebrate your courage and the progress you've made. Embrace the future with an open heart, knowing you have the tools, support, and self-awareness necessary to keep healing and thriving. Thank you for allowing this book to be part of your journey. May it always remind you of your incredible ability to grow and heal.

Thank you!

From the bottom of my heart, thank you for choosing this book. Your support is a precious gift.

If this book has touched your life or offered you any guidance, I would be deeply grateful if you could **post a review** on the platform. **Your story can be a beacon of hope for others who are on their own healing journey.** By sharing how this book has helped you, you offer encouragement and inspiration to those who might be struggling and searching for relief.

Your review not only supports independent authors like myself but also contributes to a community of hope and healing. **Your words can make a profound difference in someone else's life, showing them they are not alone and that positive change is possible.**

Thank you once again for your support and for being a vital part of this shared journey toward healing and hope.

-Stella Nash

References

Understanding the Inner Child

Cooks-Campbell, A. (2022, March 15). *How Inner Child Work Enables Healing and Playful Discovery* . Www.betterup.com. https://www.betterup.com/blog/inner-child-work

CBT, M. (2014). *My CBT* . My CBT. https://mycognitivebehavioraltherapy.com/the-inner-child-cbt

Daines, C. L., Hansen, D., Novilla, M. L. B., & Crandall, A. (2021, April 5). *Effects of Positive and Negative Childhood Experiences on Adult Family Health* . BMC Public Health. https://doi.org/10.1186/s12889-021-10732-w

Hestbech, A. M. (2018, July). *Reclaiming the Inner Child in Cognitive-Behavioral Therapy: The Complementary Model of the Personality* . American Journal of Psychotherapy. https://doi.org/10.1176/appi.psychotherapy.20180008

Ph.D, L. C. (2024, March 29). *Reparenting: Seeking Healing for Your Inner Child* . PositivePsychology.com. https://positivepsychology.com/reparenting/

Webster, E. M. (2022, February 26). *The Impact of Adverse Childhood Experiences on Health and Development in Young Children* . Global Pediatric Health. https://doi.org/10.1177/2333794x221078708

Identifying Childhood Traumas

Ackerman, C. (2017, October 26). *Writing Therapy: Using A Pen and Paper to Enhance Personal Growth* . PositivePsychology.com. https://positivepsychology.com/writing-therapy/

Gillis, K. (2022, February 19). *10 Ways Childhood Trauma Can Manifest in Adult Relationships | Psychology Today* . Www.psychologytoday.com. https://www.psychologytoday.com/us/blog/invisible-bruises/202202/10-ways-childhood-trauma-can-manifest-in-adult-relationships

Lippard, E., & Nemeroff, C. (2019, September 20). *The Devastating Clinical Consequences of Child Abuse and Neglect: Increased Disease Vulnerability and Poor Treatment Response in Mood Disorders* . American Journal of Psychiatry. https://doi.org/10.1176/appi.ajp.2019.19010020

Manifestations of Childhood Trauma in Adults — Seattle Psychiatrist . (n.d.). Seattle Anxiety Specialists, PLLC: Psychiatry & Psychology. https://seattleanxiety.com/psychiatrist/2022/5/17/manifestations-of-childhood-trauma-in-adults

Newman, K. M. (2020, August 18). *How journaling can help you in hard times* . Greater Good Magazine; The Greater Good Science Center at the University of California, Berkeley. https://greatergood.berkeley.edu/article/item/how_journaling_can_help_you_in_hard_times

Petersen, A. C., Joseph, J., & Feit, M. (2014). *Consequences of Child Abuse and Neglect* . Nih.gov; National Academies Press (US). https://www.ncbi.nlm.nih.gov/books/NBK195987/

Embracing Emotional Awareness

Ackerman, C. (2017, January 18). *22 mindfulness exercises, techniques & activities for adults (+ pdf's)* . Positive Psychology. https://positivepsychology.com/mindfulness-exercises-techniques-activities/

Emotional Awareness: Definition, Benefits & Techniques . (n.d.). Modern Recovery Services. https://modernrecoveryservices.com/wellness/coping/skills/emotional/emotional-awareness/

Gerszberg, C. O. (2022, October 13). *A Mindful Guide to Navigating Difficult Emotions* . Mindful. https://www.mindful.org/a-mindful-guide-to-navigating-difficult-emotions/

Melany. (2020, January 15). *How to Journal for Self-Awareness & Healing Emotional Wounds* . Melany Oliver. https://melany-oliver.com/journaling-selfawareness-healing-emotional-wounds/

McGowan, E. (2023, August 28). *Here's A Journal Prompt For Every Emotion You Might Be Feeling Right Now* . The Good Trade. https://www.thegoodtrade.com/features/journal-prompts/

Mari, D. (2017, October 18). *Why is understanding our emotions and feelings so important?* Counselling Psychologist | Reigate | Surrey | Online | Individual & Couples Therapy. https://www.drmarikovanen.co.uk/emotions-feelings-important/

Healing Practices and Techniques

Expressive Arts Therapy | Psychology Today . (n.d.). Www.psychologytoday.com. https://www.psychologytoday.com/us/therapy-types/expressive-arts-therapy

Griffiths, N. (2022, April 4). *30 Journal Prompts for Healing Your Inner Child and Shadow Work* . Seeking Serotonin. https://seekingserotonin.com/journal-prompts-for-inner-child-healing/

Great Valley Publishing Company, Inc. (2011). *Therapeutic Use of Expressive Arts With Children* . Socialworktoday.com. https://www.socialworktoday.com/archive/exc_020712.shtml

Raypole, C. (2020, July 8). *8 Tips for Healing Your Inner Child* . Healthline. https://www.healthline.com/health/mental-health/inner-child-healing

Sutton, J. (2022, October 8). *Inner child healing: 35 practical tools for growing beyond your past* . PositivePsychology.com. https://positivepsychology.com/inner-child-healing/

Sciandra, F. (2024, May 3). *Francesca Sciandra* . Francesca Sciandra. https://francescasciandra.com/blog/100-inner-child-journal-prompts-reparenting-for-healing-and-growth

Cultivating Self-Compassion

Crego, A., Yela, J. R., Riesco-Matías, P., Gómez-Martínez, M.-Á., & Vicente-Arruebarrena, A. (2022). *The Benefits of Self-Compassion in Mental Health Professionals: A Systematic Review of Empirical Research* . Psychology Research and Behavior Management. https://doi.org/10.2147/PRBM.S359382

Gupta, S. (2024, March 28). *5 self-compassion exercises to practice daily* . Verywell Mind. https://www.verywellmind.com/self-compassion-exercises-to-practice-daily-8619690

Moore, C. (2019, June 2). *How to practice self-compassion: 8 techniques and tips* . Positive Psychology. https://positivepsychology.com/how-to-practice-self-compassion/

Mindful Affirmations: How Positive Self-Talk Can Transform Your Life . (2024). Holstee; Holstee. https://www.holstee.com/blogs/mindful-matter/mindful-affirmations-how-positive-self-talk-can-transform-your-life?srsltid=AfmBOoqmb7W_pm6rwrgWDlLPWRWIfyzx5lxFwtOyfrqf8e4DqNrKecBg

Neff, K. (n.d.). *Self-compassion practices* . Self-Compassion. https://self-compassion.org/self-compassion-practices/

Rushforth, A., Durk, M., Gabby, Kirkman, A., Ng, F., & Kotera, Y. (2023, June 12). *Self-Compassion Interventions to Target Secondary Traumatic Stress in Healthcare Workers: A Systematic Review* . International Journal of Environmental Research and Public Health; Multidisciplinary Digital Publishing Institute. https://doi.org/10.3390/ijerph20126109

Setting Healthy Boundaries

6 Ways to Set Boundaries Without Guilt . (2022). Psychology Today. https://www.psychologytoday.com/us/blog/conquering-codependency/202208/6-ways-set-boundaries-without-guilt

Bay. (2024, July 18). *Establishing Healthy Relationship Boundaries* . Bay Area CBT Center. https://bayareacbtcenter.com/establishing-healthy-relationship-boundaries/

Lee, C. I. (2022, July 12). *Setting Boundaries Without Guilt—Is It Possible?* LA Concierge Psychologist. https://laconciergepsychologist.com/blog/setting-boundaries-without-guilt/

Martinez, J. (2024, March 29). *How To Set Boundaries With People: A Practical Guide* . Recovery Team. https://www.recoveryteam.org/how-to-set-boundaries-with-people-a-practical-guide/

Reid, S. (2024, February 5). *Setting healthy boundaries in relationships* . Help Guide. https://www.helpguide.org/articles/relationships-communication/setting-healthy-boundaries-in-relationships.htm

cmurray. (n.d.). *Healthy vs. Unhealthy Boundaries* . https://healthyrelationshipsinitiative.org/healthy-vs-unhealthy-boundaries/

Improving Relationship Dynamics

10 Expert-Backed Communication Strategies for Stronger Relationships . (n.d.). Delta Psychology. https://www.deltapsychology.com/psychology-ponderings/10-expert-backed-communication-strategies-for-stronger-relationships

Cuncic, A. (2024, February 12). *7 Active listening techniques for better communication* . Verywell Mind. https://www.verywellmind.com/what-is-active-listening-3024343

Cooks-Campbell, A. (2022, July 15). *Triggers: Learn to Recognize and Deal With Them* . BetterUp. https://www.betterup.com/blog/triggers

Gould, W. R. (2023, March 7). *Why Vulnerability in Relationships Is So Important* . Verywell Mind. https://www.verywellmind.com/why-vulnerability-in-relationships-is-so-important-5193728

Marie, S. (2022, April 18). *Vulnerability In Relationships: Benefits and Tips* . Psych Central. https://psychcentral.com/relationships/trust-and-vulnerability-in-relationships

My Partner Triggers My Trauma: Tips and Coping Strategies . (2023, February 14). Veritas Psychotherapy and Counselling. https://veritaspsychotherapy.ca/blog/my-partner-triggers-my-trauma/

Robinson, L., Segal, J., & Jaffe, J. (2021). *How attachment styles affect adult relationships* . HelpGuide.org. https://www.helpguide.org/articles/relationships-communication/attachment-and-adult-relationships.htm

What's Your Attachment Style? (2022, September 23). Cleveland Clinic. https://health.clevelandclinic.org/attachment-theory-and-attachment-styles

Developing Effective Coping Mechanisms

10 Effective Strategies to Manage Overwhelming Emotions . (2024). DBT of South Jersey. https://dbtofsouthjersey.com/how-to-manage-overwhelming-emotions/

Mayo Clinic. (2022, April 28). *Relaxation techniques: Try these steps to reduce stress* . Mayo Clinic. https://www.mayoclinic.org/healthy-lifestyle/stress-management/in-depth/relaxation-technique/art-20045368

Manzo, J. (2024, February 8). *Self-Care: A Guide to Nurturing Your Well-Being* . Primary Health Network. https://www.primary-health.net/blog/self-care-guide-to-your-well-being/

Northwestern Medicine. (2016, August 15). *Health Benefits of Having a Routine* . Northwestern Medicine; Northwestern Medicine. https://www.nm.org/healthbeat/healthy-tips/health-benefits-of-having-a-routine

Raypole, C. (2019, May 24). *30 grounding techniques to quiet distressing thoughts* . Healthline. https://www.healthline.com/health/grounding-techniques

Robinson, L. (2019, May 2). *Relaxation Techniques for Stress Relief* . HelpGuide.org. https://www.helpguide.org/articles/stress/relaxation-techniques-for-stress-relief.htm

Schuldt, W. (2022). *Grounding Techniques* . Therapist Aid. https://www.therapistaid.com/therapy-article/grounding-techniques-article

Wright, K. W. (2023, June 21). *Emotional Journaling: How to Use Journaling to Process Emotions* . Day One | Your Journal for Life. https://dayoneapp.com/blog/emotional-journaling/

Creating a Supportive Community

Building a Support Network: The Art of Cultivating Friends Who Have Your Back . (n.d.). Www.itsrichardmartinez.com. https://www.itsrichardmartinez.com/blog/building-a-support-network-the-art-of-cultivating-friends-who-have-your-back

Borges, A. (2021). *10 Online Support Groups for Anyone Struggling to Get Through 2020* . SELF. https://www.self.com/story/online-support-groups

HIAAH. (2024, July 16). *The Importance of Community in Mental Health Recovery* . Hiaah.com. https://www.hiaah.com/community-in-mental-health-recovery

Mental Health America. (2020). *Find Support Groups | Mental Health America* . Mhanational.org. https://www.mhanational.org/find-support-groups

Nedelcu Alina. (2023, May 18). *Changes in perspective: The impact of the narrative on personal development* . Medium; Medium. https://medium.com/@alinaty/changes-in-perspective-the-impact-of-the-narrative-on-personal-development-74436d3750d9

Sandberg, B., Hurmerinta, L., & Menzfeld, M. (2024, January 17). *Volunteerism and community healing* . Community Development; Routledge. https://doi.org/10.1080/15575330.2023.2301695

The Power of Shared Experiences . (n.d.). Blog.trevecca.edu. https://blog.trevecca.edu/thehill/the-power-of-shared-experiences

University at Buffalo. (2024). *Developing Your Support System* . Socialwork.buffalo.edu. https://socialwork.buffalo.edu/resources/self-care-starter-kit/additional-self-care-resources/developing-your-support-system.html

Sustaining Long-term Growth and Resilience

41 Motivation Tips to Keep You Moving Forward . (n.d.). Www.betterup.com. https://www.betterup.com/blog/how-to-stay-motivated

BookBaker. (2024). BookBaker. https://www.bookbaker.com/ar/v/Mastering-Self-Improvement-A-Comprehensive-Guide-to-Personal-Growth-Celebrating-Your-Achievements/8a84b0fc-9f9d-4a0d-9cae-3f6ed852cb52/30

Dweck, C. (2016, January 13). *What Having a "Growth Mindset" Actually Means* . Harvard Business Review. https://hbr.org/2016/01/what-having-a-growth-mindset-actually-means

Greenslade, K. (2024, May 2). *Kate Greenslade* . Kate Greenslade. https://www.onlinemindfulnesscoach.com/blog/the-importance-of-self-reflection

How to Set Professional Goals for Yourself (With 11 Examples) . (n.d.). Purdue Global. https://www.purdueglobal.edu/blog/careers/setting-professional-goals-with-examples/

Karunaratne, S. (2018, October 4). *Why You Should Be Celebrating Your Sobriety Birthday* . Eudaimonia Sober Living Homes. https://eudaimoniahomes.com/celebrate-sobriety-birthday/

Staff, M. (2024, February 25). *5 Benefits of Including Mindful Affirmations in Your Daily Routine* . Mindful. https://www.mindful.org/5-benefits-of-including-mindful-affirmations-in-your-daily-routine/

What Is a Long-term Goal and How Can I Achieve It? (n.d.). Www.betterup.com. https://www.betterup.com/blog/what-is-a-long-term-goal

About the Author

Stella Nash is a compassionate therapist, counselor, and mental health advocate who speaks from personal experience of childhood trauma. Having walked her own healing journey, she combines her deep personal insights with professional expertise to guide others in confronting past traumas and nurturing their inner child. With a warm, relatable approach, Stella inspires hope and resilience, guiding others toward transformative healing and self-discovery.

9 789334 128161

Printed at Repro India Ltd.